Barney Barrett and

Networking in English

Informal

communication

in business

Macmillan Education
4 Crinan Street
London N1 9XW
A division of Macmillan Publishers Limited
Companies and representatives throughout the world

ISBN 978-0-230-73248-3

First published 2010

Book design by Anthony Godber
Page make-up by Anne Davies
Illustrated by Martin Sanders and Gary Wing
Cover design by Andrew Oliver
Cover photograph by Photodisk

Authors' acknowledgements:
Barney Barrett would like to thank John and Mary Barrett for their love and support. Pete Sharma would like to thank María and Jade for their love and patience.

The author and publishers would like to thank the following for permission to repro-
duce their photographs:
Alamy/ Finished Camel p28mr, Peter Horree p28l; Bananastock p40 3; Brand X
Pictures p32 1; BusinessCartoons/ Morris p69 t and b; ComStock p40 4; Corbis
pp16, 36r, 38l, 38ml, 40 2; Corbis/ Alinari Archives p73 3, Corbis/ The Gallery
Collection p73 1 and 2; Digital Vision pp32 2, 40 5; Getty Images/ Ethan Miller
p36l, ImageSource pp14,40 6, 67 2, 67 3; PhotoAlto pp6, 31, 74 (all); Photodisc
p32 3; Rubberball Productions pp38r, 38mr; Stockbyte pp40 1, 46, 67 1, 70.

The author and publishers are grateful for permission reprint the following copyright
material:
Diagram from 'Riding the Waves' by Fons Trompenaars and Charles Hampden-
Turner (Nicholas Brealey Publishing, 1993) copyright © Nicholas Brealey 1993 for
UK & Commonwealth rights and McGraw Hill Companies for Rest of World rights,
reprinted by permission of both publishers.

Printed and bound in Thailand
2020 2019 2018 2017 2016
13 12 11 10 9 8 7 6 5 4

Contents

To the student

networking (noun): meeting and talking to people to discuss work or interests

Many professional people are often very good at talking about what their company does, but they may not be able to network effectively, by making small talk in the lift before a meeting or over dinner, for example. This book offers systematic coverage of networking in English. It covers survival English in common networking situations, a range of areas including grammar, vocabulary and listening, and some of the interpersonal strategies used by good native speaker and non-native speaker communicators.

What makes a good networker?

Let us look at what factors make an intermediate student a good socializer and a good communicator.

1 You are able to express yourself fairly **fluently**.
2 You have the **vocabulary** to speak about a range of topics.
3 You have reasonably accurate basic **grammar**.
4 You have fairly good **listening** skills, and have strategies to deal with problems like listening to fast speech and catching the main message.
5 You have a knowledge of the same kinds of communication **strategies** used by good native speaker communicators, such as an understanding of non-verbal communication.
6 You know the typical forms of interaction in various **social situations**, such as in a restaurant, and can use a good range of appropriate and useful phrases.
7 You speak with clear **pronunciation**.
8 You are sensitive to **cultural differences** between you and people from other parts of the world.

We have taken all these factors and created nine modules. Each module contains four units. Each unit is spread across two pages, so if you are taking a language course, it is possible for a class to cover one unit in a lesson.

It is possible to do the modules and units in any order, although the later units are more difficult than those at the beginning. The 'basics' of networking are at the start of the book. The more challenging material is at the end. This allows you to feel a sense of progression if you work through the book systematically. You can also study only the sections that you need to improve.

How do you use this book? First, complete the needs analysis on page 6 to find out which areas of socializing are most important and relevant for you. Then, you can complete your personal study plan (page 7).

Self-study

If you are not studying in a class, then you can work with the book and the audio CD. When you see a speaking activity you can usually prepare for this activity. Complete your social planner at the end of each unit you study. Cross-references guide you to other useful areas of the book.

Further resources

For further practice with English grammar, we recommend using *Intermediate Language Practice* by Michael Vince and Paul Emmerson (Macmillan Publishers, 2003).

The monolingual *Macmillan English Dictionary* (MED) is an excellent vocabulary resource for this level. An electronic version of the dictionary is available on the accompanying CD-ROM or the MED website (www.macmillandictionary.com). If you need help with your pronunciation, you can click on the icon next to a word and listen to the stress. Alternatively you can practise saying the word using the microphone, and compare your pronunciation with the original.

To the teacher

This book is for professional people and business English students who wish to improve their networking skills. It is for pre-intermediate level students, but it can also be used at intermediate level. It is designed to be used flexibly. It can be used in class as a free-standing book on a short course on socializing, or as part of a business English course. It can be used by students alone in self-study. The latter cannot participate in speaking tasks, but they can prepare for them. In one-to-one classes, the teacher can play the role of the other speaker in pairwork activities.

Syllabus

As a starting point, the authors have established the following characteristics of good socializers: reasonably accurate basic grammar; having the vocabulary to speak about a range of topics; listening skills, such as listening to fast speech and extracting the message; using the same kinds of communication strategies as good native speaker communicators; knowing schema in various situations; an adequate (intelligible) level of phonology (in both production and recognition); and sensitivity to cultural differences. Good socializers are also assumed to be fairly fluent speakers.

These factors have been used as a basis for creating the modules. Some areas of phonology have been collected in a unit in the listening skills module. Other areas of phonology are integrated where appropriate, eg past simple endings with stories. Fluency is dealt with in the many speaking activities throughout the book.

Course features

The book covers both grammar and vocabulary. The focus on grammar is for learners who may not have studied formally, who are inaccurate or whose English is rusty. In addition, a 'lexically dense' approach to socializing is taken, with two modules devoted to vocabulary.

The book is accompanied by an audio CD. The listening material contains lexis which is frequently slightly above the target level of students to ensure the dialogues are realistic and to give students practice in listening to slightly challenging material in order to prepare them for the real world. The book also draws on material outside the teaching of language. It looks at effective communication skills employed by good native speaker socializers, as well as cultural awareness training materials.

To aid the provision of context, six characters appear throughout the book. The activities and interactions of these people do not form a storyline which has to be followed chronologically. Rather, they enable students to become familiar with certain voices and personality types and to bring the social situations to life.

The book includes a range of 'tip' boxes including Networking tips and Cultural tips. Learning tip boxes provide strategies which can help autonomous study. A unique additional feature is the personalization section 'My social planner', allowing students to record useful personalized utterances. Students therefore finish the book with a bank of real phrases they can revise and use as a bridge to the real world. We suggest that after each lesson, you ask the students to spend a few minutes completing the social planner at the back of the book.

The book is heavily cross-referenced. Internal signposting refers users to other relevant parts of the syllabus.

How to use this book

If you are using the book in class, we suggest you get your students to complete the needs analysis on the next page. This will help you learn more about the students' strengths, weaknesses and social environments. Each two-page unit is designed to be used in a single lesson. Draw students' attention to the 'tip' boxes and any activities linked to them during or after a lesson. After roleplays and speaking activities, use a language feedback sheet to give learners feedback on their good use of language and their most common mistakes.

The book can be used in a self-access centre, or at home as a self-study course. The answer key is in the back, as well as the pairwork materials, listening scripts and grammar focus tables.

We hope you enjoy teaching with *Networking in English!*

Needs analysis

Tick (✔) any of the following ten statements if they are true for you.

☐ 1 My level of English is quite low and I need to cover the basics; I am worried about 'survival English' and want to study basic situations.

☐ 2 I often make basic grammar mistakes; I do not know the names of the tenses; I need to review grammar.

☐ 3 I am not a very fluent speaker; I often hesitate and pause in English, and say 'Um … er …'; I am a little shy in networking situations and I think I need more confidence when speaking.

☐ 4 I have quite a small vocabulary for my level; I can speak about my field, but not about general topics, like music and sports.

☐ 5 I am very worried about my listening; I often can't understand when other people speak quickly or if they have an accent.

☐ 6 I do not know a lot about doing business and socializing in other cultures; for example, I do not know how to interpret body language, or the way humour works in other cultures.

☐ 7 I am not sure of the phrases I need in business and social situations, like being in a restaurant or at a conference.

☐ 8 I am not sure of many of the phrases I need to do things in English, like talking about preferences or making invitations and recommendations.

☐ 9 I need to learn how to network; making small talk, keeping a conversation going and managing a conversation are quite difficult skills and I need to practise them.

☐ 10 I have problems pronouncing English; I have problems understanding native and non-native speaker accents.

What to do next?

- If you ticked 8–10 statements: We recommend that you work through the book systematically from beginning to end.
- If you ticked statement 1: Tick Module 1 on the personal study plan below.
- If you ticked statement 2: Tick Module 5 on the personal study plan below.
- If you ticked statement 3: It is better, if possible, to study in a class in order to work with other learners. If this is impossible, you should prepare the speaking activities at the end of each unit, complete your social planner and then look out for opportunities to use the language you study with other English native and non-native speakers in your usual networking situations.
- If you ticked statement 4: Tick Modules 2 and 9 on the personal study plan below.
- If you ticked statement 5: Tick Module 6 on the personal study plan below.
- If you ticked statement 6: Tick Module 8 on the personal study plan below.
- If you ticked statement 7: Choose the situations you need in Module 4 and tick them on the personal study plan below.
- If you ticked statement 8: Tick Module 3 on the personal study plan below.
- If you ticked statement 9: Tick Module 7 on the personal study plan below.
- If you ticked statement 10: Tick Module 6 Unit 4 on the personal study plan below. Also, go through the book and look at the Pronunciation tip boxes.

My personal study plan

Tick the modules and units you need to study.

I should work through the whole book systematically	☐
I should study:	
Module 1	☐
Module 2	☐
Module 3	☐
Module 4 (select the situations you need)	
Going out for a drink – study unit 1	☐
At a restaurant – study unit 2	☐
At a conference – study unit 3	☐
Meeting and greeting visitors – study unit 4	☐
Module 5	☐
Module 6	☐
Listening: pronunciation – study unit 4	☐
Module 7	☐
Module 8	☐
Module 9	☐

Now you have completed your personal study plan, you are ready to begin your course! We very much hope you enjoy using this book!

Module 1 Unit 1
Talking about you and your life

In this unit you will look at:

- appropriate topics for networking situations
- talking about yourself and people you know
- words to help you express dates and time
- talking about your life

1. Speaking – appropriate subjects

You are talking to someone for the first time. What information would you be happy to give about yourself? Rank the following categories of information 1 to 10 (1 = most happy to give this information; 10 = least happy to give this information).

Key word	**appropriate** (adjective): suitable or right for a particular situation or purpose

___ Your name
___ The company you work for
___ Your job and responsibilities
___ Where you live
___ Where you come from

___ What you studied at university
___ Your career history
___ Your ambitions and plans for the future
___ Your successes and failures
___ Your family

Compare your answer with a partner. Did you arrange the topics differently? Discuss your choices.

Cultural tip ✔ People will regard some information as more or less private depending on where they are from, for example talking about money, politics or relationships.
In your country, what subjects are inappropriate when talking to someone you do not know very well?

2a. Listening – talking about yourself (1)

1 Marc Gisset and Ingrid Kraus are having lunch after a meeting. Listen to Ingrid talking about herself to Marc. How well do they know each other? Place an X on the scale.

They have known each other ←——————→ They have only
for a long time   recently met

2b. Listening – talking about yourself (2)

1 Listen again and choose the correct answer to these questions.

1 Where is Ingrid from?   a Hamburg b Berlin
2 Where did she go to high school?   a Berlin b New Jersey
3 What did she study first at university?   a graphic design b industrial design
4 What did she design while she was at university?   a websites b posters
5 When did she become a freelance consultant?   a 2006 b 2007
6 What is her highest qualification?   a a PhD b a master's degree

3. Phrases – talking about your life

On the next page, put the stages of your life into order, from earliest to most recent. You may use some more than once. Add any that you think are missing. Then complete the sentences with your own information.

___ I got promoted to ...   ___ I moved to a different town/country
___ I graduated from university in ...   ___ I changed jobs
___ I started work in ...   ___ I went to university to study
___ I went to school in ...   ___ I was born in ...

4. Vocabulary – talking about dates and time

Use the time reference words in the box to complete the sentences about Ingrid's life and career.

for	to	since	in	from	ago	on

1 I was born in Hamburg _____ 1982.
2 I was in the US _____ 1996 _____ 1998.
3 I moved to Berlin 10 years _____ .

4 I was at university _____ 6 years.
5 I launched my business _____ 15 May 2006.
6 I've been a freelance designer _____ 2003.

5. Speaking – about yourself

Think about your life. Prepare to tell someone about yourself. Try to use the language you have learnt in this unit.

6. Vocabulary – talking about friends and family

Angie and Claire talk about their families. Use the verbs in the box to complete their answers. Make sure you put the verb into the correct form.

graduate	start	move	travel	join	do

Angie: How's your mother?

Claire: She's very well. She [1]_____ house last week.

Claire: How are your sons?

Angie: Jacob's recently [2]_____ a bank in Shanghai. David's going [3]_____ from Harvard in the fall.

Angie: How are your children?

Claire: Oh they're great. Oliver's [4]_____ well at his new school. Daisy's just [5]_____ riding lessons.

Angie: How's Robert?

Claire: Oh he's absolutely fine. He's planning to [6]_____ around Russia later this month to meet clients.

7. Speaking – people you know

Write down the names of four friends or colleagues. Work with a partner. Use the question 'How's [name]?' to ask about each person. Answer and give information about their recent or current activities.

> **Pronunciation tip** ✔ The verb 'be' and negative forms are usually contracted in the spoken form of English. For example: *I'm* from Germany. I *don't* live in Hamburg anymore.

🔊 2 Listen to these sentences with and without contractions. Which sound more natural?

8. Social planner

Now turn to page 104 and fill in the social planner with information about you and your life.

Module 1 Unit 2
Asking and answering questions

In this unit you will look at:

- question words
- making and answering questions
- getting to know someone
- turning the question around

1. Question words

Match the question words (1–8) to the descriptions of their use (a–h).

1	what	**a**	about the length of time
2	which	**b**	about things, actions or ideas
3	when	**c**	what time something happens
4	where	**d**	about the number of people or things
5	who	**e**	about people
6	why	**f**	for a specific choice from a limited number of possibilities
7	how long	**g**	about places
8	how many	**h**	the reason for something

2a. Grammar – making questions

Reorder the words to make questions.

1 Where from you are? *Where are you from?*
2 What you do do?
3 Who for work do you?
4 How your job been long have in you?

5 When company the you join did?
6 Where based you are?
7 Why you your join company did?
8 How many department people your in work?

 Pronunciation tip Like many other languages, it is possible to make questions in English by using a statement with rising intonation at the end.

For example: You're from Germany? You went to university in the US?

However, it is often clearer to use the full question, like those in exercise 2a, where the stress falls on the main verb. For example: Where do you **come** from? Who do you **work** for?

 3 Listen to these sentences and try to repeat the intonation and stress.

2b. Speaking – answering questions

How would you answer the questions in 2a?
Work with a partner to ask and answer them.

3a. Listening – getting to know each other (1)

 4 Now listen to Brad J Ruby talking to Ashok Patel before a meeting. Which country are they in?

3b. Listening – getting to know each other (2)

4 We use *which* to make questions when we are asking about a specific choice from a limited number of possibilities. Listen to Brad and Ashok again and answer these *which* questions.

1 Which places did Brad visit on his first trip to India? **a** The Taj Mahal **b** Delhi **c** Mumbai
2 In which US city did Ashok go to university? **a** Los Angeles **b** Boston
3 Which European cities is Brad going to visit on this trip? **a** Berlin **b** Paris **c** London
4 In which country was Ashok's wife born? **a** Scotland **b** India

3c. Phrases – turning the question around

Turning the question around is an easy way of moving the conversation forward. For example:

Ashok: So, do you travel a lot for business, Brad?

Brad: At the moment, yes. People in my industry prefer face-to-face meetings. How about you?

Ashok: I only really travel for conferences. Us IT people are quite happy to communicate electronically.

4 During their conversation Brad and Ashok use this expression three times to turn the question around. Listen again. What are they talking about each time?

4a. Grammar – questions (1)

Correct the mistakes in these questions.

1 Where you come from?
2 How much time have you lived in Berlin?
3 You are married?
4 Have you children?
5 Where do you go on holiday last year?
6 Do you have got your new car yet?

4b. Grammar – questions (2)

Match the questions in 4a to the correct responses below.

a We spent three weeks scuba diving in the Maldives. _____
b Yes, my son is six and my daughter is eight. _____
c I'm from Hamburg in the north of Germany. _____
d No. My partner lives in New York. _____
e No, it's being delivered sometime next week. _____
f About 2 years now. _____

5. Speaking – a first conversation

Work with a partner. Student A has just flown in for a meeting. Student B is the host. Use the prompts in the grid to guide your conversation. Don't forget to turn the question around.

> **Key word**
>
> **host** (noun): someone who invites people to a meal or party, or to stay in their home
>
> **guest** (noun): someone who you have invited to your home, for a party or a meal, or to stay the night

Student B starts.

How / journey? ▶	your first time? ▶	How long / stay? ▼
▼ travel a lot?	◀ business or holiday?	◀ Where / last holiday?
What / think of? ▶	What / free time? ▶	do any sports?

6. Social planner

Now turn to the social planner on page 104 for some more practice on useful networking questions.

Module 1 Unit 3
Talking about your company and business

In this unit you will look at:

- introducing and describing your company
- giving facts and figures about your company
- correcting and clarifying information
- some useful business collocations
- talking about the performance of your company

1. Phrases – introducing your company

Look at Marc's two responses to the question *'Who do you work for?'*. Which answer is better? Why?

1 I work for Central International.
2 I'm the managing director of a French engineering company called Central International. We work with construction companies all over the world to design and build skyscrapers and stadiums.

Imagine someone asks you who you work for. Use Marc's second answer above as a template.

For more vocabulary for talking about your company, see Module 2 Unit 4.

2. Vocabulary – describing a company

Match the business words (1–8) to the correct definitions (a–h).

1	workforce	a	a person or company that buys goods or services
2	market	b	something that is made or grown in large quantities so that it can be sold
3	product	c	the value of the goods and services that a company sells in a particular period of time
4	turnover	d	the money that remains after you have paid all your business costs
5	profit	e	the total number of people who work in a particular company
6	customer	f	someone who pays for the services of a professional person such as a doctor or lawyer
7	service	g	a particular place or group of people that a product is sold to
8	client	h	work, help or advice provided by a business or organization

3a. Listening – giving facts and figures about your company

5 Listen to Brad and Ashok talking about Ashok's company. Fill in the information about the company.

IOL TECHNOLOGIES				
Markets:	Workforce:	Turnover:	Profit:	Number of clients:
_____	_____	_____	_____	_____

3b. Correcting and clarifying information

5 Listen again. What does Brad misunderstand? How does Ashok clarify the figure?

> *Pronunciation tip* ✔ The difference between the pronunciation of numbers such as 16 and 60 is the stress pattern of the word. For the numbers 13–19, the second syllable is stressed.
> For example: six*teen*. For the numbers 20, 30, 40, etc, the first syllable is stressed. For example: *six*ty.
>
> 6 Listen to the pairs of numbers. Can you tell the difference?

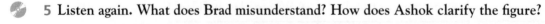

Cultural tip It is not always appropriate to talk a lot about business in a social situation. When do you think a 'topic not related to business' might be better?

4. Speaking – giving facts and figures about your company

Choose four items from the list and write down the figure for your company.

number of employees	last year's profit
position in the market / market share	number of customers / clients
number of products / services	number of subsidiaries
last year's turnover	number of offices around the world

Work with a partner, using 'how much' or 'how many' questions to find out their figures.

5a. Vocabulary – business collocations (1)

Match the verbs 1–8 to the words a–h to make some common business collocations.

1	lay	5	win	a the budget	e a subsidiary
2	make	6	hire	b new employees	f contingency plans
3	recruit	7	set up	c a contract	g a contract
4	increase	8	lose	d people off	h staff

5b. Vocabulary – business collocations (2)

Look at Angie's conversation with Claire and Ashok. Use some of the collocations in 5a to fill in the gaps. Make sure you put the verbs into the correct form.

Angie: How's business?

Claire: Really exciting. HR are very busy. The company ¹ _won_ a big _contract_ in New Delhi so the board have decided to ² _____ a small _____ in India. They want me to ³ _____ about a hundred new _____ over there very quickly so I had to ask them to ⁴ _____ my department's _____ .

Ashok: Not as good as last year. The downturn in the US economy has hit us badly. We had to ⁵ _____ _____ in Boston. We ⁶ _____ _____ a couple of years ago in case this situation happened, so we've managed to keep our prices competitive and we're sure we won't ⁷ _____ any _____ .

6a. Vocabulary – commenting on the performance of your company

'How's business?' is a more informal way of asking about a company's performance. Decide how strong these responses are using the relevant symbol: ++ (very positive), + (positive), ⁻ (negative), ⁻⁻ (very negative). There are at least two examples for each strength of response.

1 Not as good as last year.
2 Pretty good considering the high price of oil.
3 Best not to talk about it.
4 Picking up.
5 Better than last year.

6 We're in a bit of trouble at the moment.
7 Really exciting at the moment.
8 Not great.
9 Not bad.
10 Doing really well actually.

6b. Speaking – reporting on the performance of your company

In pairs, tell each other about the past and future performance of your business. Use the information from your respective charts (student A on page 80, student B on page 82) to answer.

7. Social planner

Now turn to the social planner on page 104 and write some sentences about your company.

Module 1 Unit 4
Greetings, introductions and goodbyes

In this unit you will look at:

- greeting people
- introducing other people
- answers to 'How are you?'
- saying goodbye

1a. Listening – greetings

7 Listen to three pairs of people greeting each other. Match them to the correct description of the relationship.

1 The people are friends. _____
2 The people are meeting each other for the first time. _____
3 The people see each other regularly. _____

1b. Phrases – greeting people

7 Listen again, and tick (✔) the greetings you hear. What are the differences in their use?

| How do you do? | Hi | Morning | Glad to meet you | Good morning |
| Nice to hear from you | Good afternoon | Hello | Good evening | Pleased to meet you |

> **Vocabulary tip** ✔ When does 'Good morning' change to 'Good afternoon'? In the UK and USA, it happens at midday. In other countries it can be as late as 2pm. Similarly, some people use 'Good evening' only after office hours; others after sunset. (Note: 'Good night' is used to say goodbye in the evening.)

2a. Phrases – introducing other people

Look at these two dialogues in which Ingrid introduces Ashok to Marc. Reorder the lines.

Dialogue 1

a Ingrid: Good morning Ashok. __1__
b Ashok: I'm very pleased to meet you too, Mr Gisset. _____
c Ingrid: May I introduce you to Marc Gisset from Central International. Marc, this is Ashok Patel from IOL Technologies in Mumbai. _____
d Marc: It is a pleasure to meet you Mr Patel. _____
e Ashok: Good morning Ingrid. _____

Dialogue 2

a Ingrid: Hey Ashok! Have you met Marc Gisset before? __1__
b Marc: Very well, thank you. And you? _____
c Ashok: Nice to meet you too Marc. How are you? _____
d Ingrid: I'll introduce you. Marc, this is Ashok Patel from Mumbai. _____
e Marc: Nice to meet you Ashok. _____
f Ashok: Hi Ingrid. No, I don't think I have. _____
g Ashok: I'm well thanks. _____

Which of the two dialogues is more formal?

> **Cultural tip** ✔ The social rules about whether you address someone using their title and family name, eg Mr Ruby, or their first name, eg Brad, vary from country to country. Often it is better to be more formal at the beginning and only use a person's first name if they invite you to do so, eg 'Please call me Brad'.

2b. Speaking – making introductions

Work in pairs. Student A turn to page 80, student B to page 82. Do the activity.

3. Phrases – answers to 'How are you?'

There are a number of possible answers to the question *'How are you?'*. Match the phrases to their position on the scale.

Not great _____   Terrible _____   Not too good _____   Great __*1*__
Good _____   Fine _____   Pretty good _____   Very well _____

> **Cultural tip** ✔ 'OK' is not necessarily a positive answer, particularly in British English. It can mean that although you are not unwell, you would prefer to feel better than you do.

4a. Listening – saying goodbye

🔘 **8** Listen to these different ways of saying goodbye. Fill in the gaps.

Dialogue 1
Brad: OK Ashok, I'll [1]_____.
Ashok: [2]_____ Brad. See [3]_____.
Brad: Ciao.

Dialogue 2
Claire: Well, Angie, it was [4]_____.
Angie: [5]_____Claire. It was wonderful to catch up.
Claire: I'll see you again before you fly back to Hong Kong.
Angie: Of course. [6]_____ for now.
Claire: [7]_____. Bye-bye.

Dialogue 3
Ingrid: It was [8]_____, Mrs Wong-Smith.
Angie: It was nice meeting you too, Ms Kraus. [9]_____ for coming.
Ingrid: [10]_____.
Angie: Goodbye. Have [11]_____.

4b. Matching – hellos and goodbyes

🔘 **7** Listen again to the greeting dialogues from exercise 1a. Then match them to the goodbye dialogues in 4a.

5. Speaking – greetings and introductions

How would you greet the other person and introduce yourself when meeting:

- your new boss?
- an old friend you haven't seen for years?
- a regular supplier?
- the wife of a business contact, for the first time?
- a potential client at a conference?
- a colleague from another office?

Work with a partner and roleplay each situation.

See also Module 1 Unit 2, Module 7 Unit 1 and Module 7 Unit 4.

6. Social planner

Now turn to the social planner on page 104 for more practice on hellos and goodbyes.

Module 2 Unit 1
Talking about free time and travel

In this unit you will look at:

- adverbs of frequency
- hobbies and free time activities
- collocations with do/play/go
- talking about your hobbies
- talking about holidays and travel
- planning a company weekend

1. Quiz – your work-life balance

How good is your work-life balance? Complete the quiz and calculate your score. Then go to page 97 for feedback. Compare your answer with a partner. How can you improve your lifestyle?

Fit for work?

1 How often do you take regular weekend breaks?
Frequently = 3 points   Occasionally = 1 point   Never = 0 points

2 How sporty are you?
Very = 3 points   A bit = 1 point   Not at all = 0 points

3 How often do you go out with your colleagues/friends after work?
Usually = 3 points   Sometimes = 1 point   Never = 0 points

4 How often do you work overtime or take work home with you at the weekend?
Hardly ever = 3 points   Sometimes = 1 point   Often = 0 points

5 How often do you eat your lunch at your desk?
Never = 3 points   Occasionally = 1 point   Frequently = 0 points

---

Grammar tip   There are a number of adverbs in English used to describe frequency: 'how often' we do things. Some examples (from most to least frequent) are: always, usually, often, frequently, sometimes, occasionally, rarely, hardly ever, never. Note the position of the adverbs in the following sentences: *I **never** miss a deadline/You are **often** right/He has **always** liked me.*

2a. Vocabulary – hobbies

Choose ten different letters of the alphabet. In three minutes try to write down as many games or hobbies as you can beginning with these letters.

2b. Collocations – do/play/go

Match each noun to the correct verb.

do	parachuting	fishing	swimming	tai chi	chess
play	scuba diving	yoga	gardening	pilates	jogging
go	computer games	cards	the guitar	sport	squash

2c. Speaking – talking about your hobbies

Compare and discuss your list of hobbies from 2a and 2b with a partner. Which do you do?

For further practice, see Module 9 Unit 2 Talking about sport.

3a. Listening – talking about holidays and travel (1)

9 **Listen to Angie, Brad, Ingrid and Ashok talking about their holidays. Who is talking about:**

1 a country they have visited and enjoyed?
2 countries they visit regularly?

3 a country they would love to visit?
4 a business trip?

Vocabulary tip Three words commonly confused by English learners are 'trip', 'journey' and 'travel'. Look at the definitions below to see the difference between them:

trip (noun): an occasion when you go somewhere and come back again
journey (noun): an occasion when you travel from one place to another
travel (verb): to go from one place to another or visit different places

3b. Listening – talking about holidays and travel (2)

9 **Listen again and answer the questions.**

1 What must Angie have when flying over Africa?
2 What didn't Brad like about Mexico?

3 Why does Ingrid holiday closer to home now?
4 When does Ashok plan to visit Paris?

3c. Speaking – my travels

How about you? First, mark the following numbers on the map. Then, explain your choices to a partner. Use expressions from the listening in 3a and 3b.

1 = a country you have visited and enjoyed
2 = a country you visit regularly
3 = a country you would love to visit
4 = a country you have visited on business

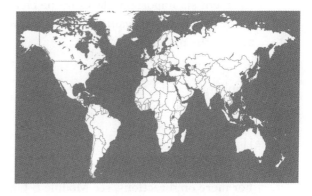

4. Planning a company weekend

Your company wants to organize a weekend away for all staff as a reward for their hard work. You have been asked to plan this trip. First, use the map in 3c and choose a suitable location. Then, choose the type of conference you prefer from one of the advertisements below. Discuss your preference with a partner. Can you agree on a suitable choice?

1 *Business adventure:* Outdoor team-building activities. Work together on challenging outdoor tasks. Build that bridge — climb that mountain.

2 LIFE COACHING
A wide choice of seminars including: motivation techniques; managing time; and effective people skills.

3 Business alternative
Take a relaxing break from the pressures of the office. De-stress. Yoga. Mineral baths. Swimming. Gym. Massage.

5. Social planner

Now turn to the social planner on page 105 and write sentences about your hobbies and travel preferences.

Module 2 Unit 2
Talking about your town and country

In this unit you will look at:

- vocabulary of towns and places
- recommending things to do
- talking about towns and countries
- talking and writing about your country

1. Vocabulary – places

Arrange the following places in order of size. 1 = biggest, 6 = smallest.

county _____   continent _1_   town _____   village _____   city _____   country _____

2a. Listening – finding places on a map (1)

10 **Listen to Ashok talking to Marc about Edinburgh. Tick (✔) the subjects that are mentioned.**

statues   castles   museums   cinemas   palaces   parks   zoos   restaurants

2b. Listening – finding places on a map (2)

10 **Look at the map of Edinburgh. Numbers 1–6 represent six important places in the city. Listen to the conversation again and write the numbers next to the places below.**

Royal Mile _____
Edinburgh Castle _____
Princes Street _____
Scott's Monument _____
Holyrood Palace _____
Royal Museum of Scotland _____

For more on directions, see Module 6 Unit 3.

2c. Phrases – recommendations

Put the words in the correct order to make sentences.

1 Street must visit You Princes.
2 Mile miss Don't the Royal.
3 the visiting I'd recommend Museum Royal.
4 see famous You the should statue.

10 **Listen again to check your answers.**

For more on making recommendations, see Module 3 Unit 3.

3a. Vocabulary – your town

Complete the sentences with the missing words.

ruins	souvenir	district	fair	population	speciality

1 People come here from around the country for the annual summer _____ .
2 The _____ is about 200,000.
3 The local _____ is fish.
4 This pottery would be a lovely _____ of your visit.
5 There are some old Roman _____ to the west of the city.
6 You have to stay in the canal _____ – it's one of the nicest parts of town.

3b. Writing – your town

Think of a town in your country. What is special or interesting about it? What would you recommend doing there? Complete the sentence beginnings to give recommendations about the town.

You must …   Don't miss …   I'd recommend …   You should …

4a. Listening – visiting different countries (1)

11 Listen to four people talking about different countries. Write down the names of the countries.

1 _____   2 _____   3 _____   4 _____

4b. Listening – visiting different countries (2)

11 All of these topics are mentioned in the listening. Listen again and note down which speaker (1, 2, 3 or 4) mentions each one. There is only one answer for each topic.

festivals _____   currency _____   local speciality _____   trains _____
souvenirs _____   best time to visit _____   temples _____   the largest town _____

> **Networking tip** ✔ Socializing provides a great opportunity to find out more about the famous people from your host's country. Ask further questions such as: 'Tell me a little more about him/her'; 'When was he/she alive?'; 'Remind me what he/she was famous for'. If you haven't heard of that person, good phrases to use are 'that rings a bell' and 'I've definitely heard the name…'

4c. Writing & speaking – famous people

Look at the names of famous people in the box. Where are they from?

| Michelangelo   George Best   Eva Perón   Martina Navratilova   Nostradamus   Desmond Tutu |

Work with a partner. Student A should begin by picking a name from the box and pretending to be from that country, and student B should be the visitor. Roleplay the situation. For example:

Student A: I'm sure you've heard of Michelangelo, the famous painter? He was born here.
Student B: Yes, I think so. Didn't he paint the Sistine Chapel?

Then change roles for each new name.

5a. Talking about your country

Choose a country you have visited. Complete the fact sheet for this country.

5b. Speaking – information exchange

In pairs, tell each other about your countries. Did you learn anything new?

6. Social planner

Write some sentences about your own country in the social planner on page 105.

Fact sheet
Country: _____
Capital: _____
Currency: _____
Sightseeing highlight(s):
_____
Another town to visit:
_____
Famous person:
_____
Famous national dish:
_____
Souvenir 'must have':
_____
Any local specialities:
_____

Module 2 Unit 3
Food and drink

In this unit you will look at:

- types of food and drink
- talking about tastes and preferences
- meal courses
- describing food
- ordering drinks
- creating a menu

1. Vocabulary – food

Draw a table with four different headings: *vegetables, fruit, meat and poultry* and *fish and seafood*. Then write the names of the different kinds of food in the correct categories.

cherry	strawberry	mango	pork	lamb
peach	peppers	salmon	mushroom	cod
prawns	mussels	chicken	pineapple	broccoli
turkey	tuna	lettuce	potato	beef

2a. Listening – eating preferences (1)

12 Brad and Marc are eating in a restaurant. Listen to their conversation. Who has the healthier diet?

2b. Listening – eating preferences (2)

12 Listen again. Decide whether the statements are true or false.

1 Brad still eats burgers.
2 Marc thinks he could live without cheese.
3 Brad eats five portions of fruit and vegetables every day.
4 Marc wants to order more wine.

2c. Speaking – your eating preferences

Do you:
- choose healthy options?
- eat fried foods?
- have small portions?
- prefer mild or hot dishes?
- avoid greasy or fatty foods?
- try exotic foods?
- skip meals?
- like sauces?

Compare your eating preferences with a partner.

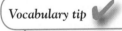 **Vocabulary tip** Be careful! The adjective 'hot' can have two meanings when talking about food: (1) very high in temperature or (2) containing a lot of spices.

3a. Vocabulary – courses

Put the following 'courses' (parts of a meal) in the order in which they are served.

coffee _____ dessert _____ aperitif _____ starter _____ main course _____

3b. Speaking – describing food

1 lasagne	fried rice	chicken tikka curry	sushi	moussaka	paella	pizza	kebab	burrito

2 sweet	bitter	greasy	creamy	spicy	bland	rich	salty	mild	it's made with ...

Choose two dishes from box 1. Then use words from box 2 to describe them.

For further practice, see Module 4 Unit 2, Module 3 Unit 1, Module 3 Unit 3 and Module 3 Unit 4.

4a. Vocabulary – types of drink

Fill in the spaces with a word from the box to create word partnerships related to drinks.

wine	beer	juice	water	~~drink~~

1 hot / cold / soft / fizzy _____*drink*_____
2 orange / grapefruit / tomato / apple / pineapple / cranberry _____
3 still / sparkling / mineral / tap / tonic / iced _____
4 red / white / dry / house / sweet / sparkling _____
5 Czech / bottled / non-alcoholic / a pint of / a half of _____

4b. Phrases – ordering drinks

At the bar in the UK, you might hear this expression when someone offers to buy a 'round' of drinks for the people they are with. Match the statements (1–7) to the responses (a–g).

'It's my round. What would you like?'

1 Lager, please.
2 Just a mineral water.
3 What juices have they got?
4 What kind of beers do they have?
5 Nothing alcoholic for me, thanks.
6 White wine please, John.
7 Gin and tonic, please.

a Oh, I'm sorry. I forgot you were driving.
b Ice and lemon?
c Well, the local bitter is wonderful.
d Do you prefer sweet or dry?
e Half or a pint?
f Sparkling or still?
g Apple, orange or mango, I think.

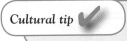
Cultural tip In the UK people ask for 'a pint' or 'a half (pint)' when they order beer, lager, bitter or cider. A litre is about 1.75 pints. It is also possible to order 'a bottle' of beer, lager, bitter or cider.

4c. Speaking – your order

What would you order if you were at the bar with a colleague or business contact? How would you order it? Use the language in exercises 4a and 4b to help you prepare your order.

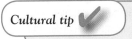
Cultural tip People from different cultures have different rules and customs when it comes to alcohol; remember to be particularly sensitive to cultures where drinking is not permitted.

For further practice with drinks, see Module 4 Unit 1.

5a. Writing – creating a menu

You are going to invite some classmates to your house for dinner. Create the food and drinks menu using the headings 'drinks', 'starters', 'main courses' and 'desserts'. Try to include local dishes where possible, and remember: one guest is a vegetarian.

5b. Speaking – roleplay

Roleplay the first five minutes of the same meal with a partner: you are the host and your partner is the guest. Remember to describe the dishes, make recommendations and find out what your guests would like to drink. Then change roles for your partner's menu.

For further practice, see Module 3 Unit 1 and Module 3 Unit 3.

6. Social planner

Now turn to the social planner on page 105 and write about your food and drink preferences.

Module 2 Unit 4
Talking about jobs and work

In this unit you will look at:

- adjectives and nouns associated with work
- job titles and functions
- types of jobs and job adverts
- talking about jobs

1a. Vocabulary – adjectives associated with work

The following words can all be used to describe jobs. Which are positive and which are negative?

| challenging | demanding | glamorous | repetitive | rewarding | stressful |

1b. Reading – a day in the life

Read the four extracts below and decide who:

1 works in personnel
2 didn't like their first job
3 has never had one permanent employer
4 doesn't like overseas travel
5 runs a team
6 sometimes stays late at the office
7 drives to work
8 enjoys the flexibility of not having fixed work times

A day in the life of ...

Marc: As you know, our firm specializes in design and construction. My job is quite challenging. The day begins quite early: 6.00am usually. I enjoy the drive to the office. I must say that I am often away and the travel is quite stressful, especially being away from my family for long periods. On the other hand, it is pretty rewarding when we win a major contract, and there's real satisfaction when the job is done.

Claire: I love being in human resources. It's right at the heart of the company. I start at 8.00, but sometimes I go into the office mid-morning and stay later. It all depends on what's on the agenda for that day. My job can sometimes be quite glamorous. The perks are fantastic: car, pension, life insurance, bonuses. I don't think anyone in this sector can complain about the conditions.

Ashok: My first job was in the family restaurant. It was quite repetitive. I started early and finished late, and the wage was extremely low. I consider myself a pretty hard-working guy, but I was often quite bored there. I'm glad I've managed to start up my own company, where I'm responsible for a thriving and dynamic team. The job is demanding and we work long hours but that's how you grow a company.

Ingrid: I always wanted to do something creative, you know. I wanted a career but I enjoy being a freelancer. In fact, I've never been an employee. I've always worked for myself. No one tells me when to get up and when to finish – I think if you work for yourself, you work harder. The disadvantages are that I'm always looking for the next job. On the other hand, I have a lot of freedom and I love the variety.

1c. Vocabulary – nouns associated with work

All of the words in the box appear in the article. Look up any that you don't know in the dictionary.

| agenda | bonus | career | conditions | contract | employee | firm |
| freelancer | perks | pension | salary | wage | freedom | satisfaction |

1d. Writing & speaking – your job

Create sentences about your job, using the language in exercises 1a–c.

> Cultural tip   Generally, it is not acceptable to ask someone directly how much money they make.

2a. Listening – job titles

 13 Listen to an introductory speech to a group of new employees. Make five job titles that you hear by matching a word or phrase in the left box to one in the right box.

Chief Payroll Finance Head of Research and	Development manager IT director Executive Officer clerk

2b. Phrases – job functions

Match the sentence halves to make complete sentences about job functions.

1 It's a great company to work …
2 Maria Wong is in charge …
3 The sales team all deal …
4 They answer …
5 Carl Wiseman works …
6 Jane's responsible …
7 He needs to speak to you about filling …
8 You get used …

a … with different tasks.
b … for advertising.
c … alongside Jane Robson.
d … to Lynette Strong.
e … to doing quite a few different jobs.
f … of the department.
g … in a joining form.
h … for.

 13 Listen again to the introductory speech to check your answers.

3a. Vocabulary – jobs

Look at the jobs in the box. Then look at the job adverts and decide which job each one describes.

call centre assistant	lorry driver	auditor	advertising executive	stockbroker	Web designer
careers adviser	chef	engineer	air traffic controller	trainee manager	personal assistant

1 Exciting opportunity working as a PA to the Managing Director.

3 Knowledge of HTML essential. Send CV and covering letter.

2 Help others to find their chosen job. Call Simon on 0800 156 743.

4 Good telephone manner required. Flexible hours. Overtime available.

3b. Writing – job adverts

Pick three jobs from exercise 3a that weren't advertised. Write a short advert for each one.

4. Writing & speaking – your dream job

What do you think would be a 'dream' job? Add three dream jobs to the list in 3a. Pick one.
What adjectives would you use to describe the job? What are the conditions like?
What are you responsible for? Write a description of your dream job. Then describe it to a partner – can they guess which job it is?

5. Social planner

Now turn to the social planner on page 105 and write some sentences about your own job.

Module 3 Unit 1
Likes, dislikes and preferences

In this unit you will look at:

• saying what you like and dislike   • giving preferences   • expressing dislikes politely

1.   What do you like?

Choose two of these topics and discuss your likes, dislikes and preferences with a partner.

1   travelling for business   3   negotiating with customers/clients
2   entertaining customers/clients   4   winter holidays

2.   Phrases – expressing likes and dislikes

Complete the phrases in the scale using the words in the box.

+ 1 I _____ it.
  2 I like it _____ . / I _____ like it.
  3 I _____ like it.
  4 I like it _____ .
  5 It's _____ . / It's _____ special.
  6 I _____ it very much.
  7 I _____ it at all.
− 8 I _____ it.

hate	don't like	OK	really
don't like	a little	love	
a lot	quite	nothing	

 Pronunciation tip ✔   When we modify a word such as 'like', we usually put emphasis on the modifying word: I like Indian food **a lot**. / I **really** like basketball. / I **don't** like business lunches.

 14 Listen to the sentences and try to repeat them.

3.   Speaking – likes / dislikes list

Make a list of your favourite food, the sports you enjoy playing or watching and your favourite films. Work with a partner and compare your lists. What do you like and dislike on your partner's list?

Food	Sports	Films

For more related vocabulary, see Module 2 Unit 3, Module 9 Unit 2 and Module 9 Unit 1.

4a.   Listening – giving preferences (1)

 15 Listen to Angie and Marc talking about travel. Who likes travelling the most?

4b. Listening – giving preferences (2)

15 Listen again. In each question below, which of the three statements is NOT correct?

1 Marc dislikes travelling for work because:
a he does not like flying.
b he has no time to be a tourist.
c he does not like foreign food.

2 When he has a holiday, Marc likes to:
a stay at home and go riding.
b go skiing with his daughters.
c visit New York.

3 Angie likes Shanghai because:
a the people are very optimistic.
b she has lots of friends there.
c it's closer to Hong Kong.

4 Angie prefers Shanghai to New York because:
a New York is too polluted.
b Shanghai is exciting at the moment.
c Shanghai will soon be more important for business.

5. Phrases – expressing preferences

Angie and Marc are planning an evening out. Fill in the gaps with a phrase from the box.

| It depends | Do you like | Me too | We could go | I'd definitely prefer | I'd prefer | Which would you prefer |

Marc: ¹_____ to the opera tomorrow evening.
Angie: I do like opera but I think ²_____ something less serious.
Marc: ³_____ theatre?
Angie: Yes, I like theatre a lot. I wanted to be an actress when I was younger but my mother refused to allow it.
Marc: Well, there's a Shakespeare on at the Theatre Royal or a new comedy at the Workshop Theatre.
⁴_____ ?
Angie: ⁵_____ . Which Shakespeare play is it?
Marc: Let's see. *Titus Andronicus.*
Angie: Oh no, that's a horrible play. Too much blood and guts for me. If that's the case,
⁶_____ to go and see the comedy.
Marc: ⁷_____ . I really don't like tragedies. I'll book a couple of tickets for the comedy.

6. Phrases – expressing dislikes politely

Match the direct comments on the left to the more polite phrases on the right.

1 Foreign food is awful.
2 Yuck! How can you drink milky tea?
3 Teams are such a waste of time!
4 Your proposal is a disaster.
5 It's so cold in your country.

a I'm afraid we're not convinced by your proposal.
b I'm sorry, but I don't like tea with milk.
c I prefer warmer weather.
d I prefer French food.
e I prefer to work on my own.

Underline the language which is used to make the sentences more polite.

7. Speaking – talking about preferences

Which do you prefer and why? Discuss with a partner.

- living in the city or the country
- working alone or in a team
- holidaying abroad or in your own country
- meetings in the office or over lunch
- watching sport at the stadium or on TV
- communicating by email or telephone

8. Social planner

Now turn to page 106 and fill in the social planner with your likes, dislikes and preferences.

Module 3 Unit 2
Invitations: accepting and declining

In this unit you will look at:
- making an invitation
- accepting an invitation
- declining an invitation
- responding to a declined invitation

1. Invitations

What sort of invitations do you make and receive in your business life?

Invitations to:
- go to lunch or dinner?
- go out for a drink to a bar or pub?
- sporting or cultural events?

Are you inviting or being invited by:
- customers or clients?
- suppliers?
- colleagues?

What makes you accept or decline these invitations?

2. Making and accepting an invitation

Put this short conversation between Claire and Brad into the correct order.

a Claire: We're going to try that new restaurant tonight. Do you want to come with us? __1__

b Brad: Cool. I'll see you at seven thirty. _____

c Claire: The Thai one by the river. _____

d Brad: Sorry, which restaurant is that? _____

e Claire: The table is booked for eight. We'll pick you up at half seven if that's OK. _____

f Brad: Yeah, I know the one you mean. That's great. I love Thai food. What time? _____

3a. Phrases – making an invitation

Use _would_ or _do_ to complete these invitation phrases.

1 How _____ you like to have lunch?

2 _____ you want to go for a coffee?

3 _____ you fancy coming to the cinema tonight?

4 _____ you want to come along to the match?

3b. Phrases – accepting an invitation

Now match these acceptances to the invitations in 3a. Write the correct invitation number in each space.

a I'd love to. What's on? ___

b Yes please. Is it Chelsea-Arsenal? ___

c Sure, I could do with a double espresso. ___

d Thanks, I would. Let me just finish this. ___

For more on making future arrangements, see Module 5 Unit 4.

4a. Phrases – declining an invitation

For each invitation (1–3), choose which of the three ways of declining (a, b or c) is NOT polite.

1 _Ashok: How would you like to come to a cricket match on Wednesday?_
   Angie: a I'm sorry, I'd love to but I can't make Wednesday.
            b Not really, I find cricket so boring!
            c That's kind of you but I have to be in Munich on Wednesday.

2 _Claire: Ashok, would you like to join us? We're going to a steak house for dinner later this evening._
   Ashok: a It sounds like fun but I can't eat beef. It's against my religion.
            b I would, but I've already accepted another invitation for tonight unfortunately.
            c Thank you very much but I need to get an early night.

3 Brad: *We're going to the pub after the meeting. Do you want to come along?*
   Marc: a *Not today, I'm afraid. I need to phone my wife and finish off some paperwork.*
   b *No thanks. I'm sorry but I can't stand any more of that warm beer.*
   c *Thank you for the invitation but my flight is at six. I have to go straight to the airport.*

Cultural tip In many countries, if you decline an invitation it is considered polite to explain why you can't accept. There are several examples of this in exercise 4a. Can you think of any others?

4b. Phrases – responding to a declined invitation

Which of these responses to a declined invitation are appropriate?

1 Another time maybe.   3 That's a pity.   5 That's a shame.
2 Suit yourself.   4 I don't care.   6 Whatever.

5a. Listening – inviting someone over (1)

16 **Listen to Claire and Ingrid. What are they talking about? Who is going to be there?**

5b. Listening – inviting someone over (2)

16 **Listen again and choose the correct answer to each of these questions.**

1 How many times has Ingrid been to Claire's house?
   a She's been there once before.
   b She's never been there.
   c She's been there many times.
2 When is the invitation for?
   a Thursday afternoon.
   b Thursday at eleven.
   c Thursday evening.
3 What time is dinner?
   a Eleven.
   b Eight.
   c Seven thirty.

4 What does Claire suggest Ingrid brings?
   a A bottle of wine or some chocolates.
   b Something special from Germany.
   c Nothing.
5 Where has Ingrid met Angie Wong-Smith?
   a In London.
   b In Hong Kong.
   c They haven't met before.
6 How is Ingrid getting to Claire's house?
   a By car.
   b By train and then by taxi.
   c By taxi from her house.

Cultural tip Do people invite colleagues and associates to their home in your country? If so, what are typical gifts or customs? And what would be the correct time to arrive for a dinner starting at 8pm?

Vocabulary tip Remember that in English the 24-hour clock is not used when speaking. Instead, people say the abbreviations 'am' and 'pm' – or the phrases 'in the morning', 'in the afternoon', 'in the evening' and 'at night' – after the time. For example: '7.30am' or 'seven thirty in the morning'.

6. Speaking – accepting and declining invitations

Student A turn to page 80, student B page 82. Take it in turns to invite your partner. Accept or decline the invitation using the information. Alternatively write an email response to the invitation.

7. Social planner

Now use the social planner on page 106 to practise making, accepting and declining invitations.

Module 3 Unit 3
Making requests, offers and recommendations

In this unit you will look at:

- making requests
- talking about problems
- offering a solution
- offering to help someone
- making recommendations
- what to say when you can't help

1. Help!

What is the problem in each picture? How would you request help? How would you offer to help?

2a. Phrases – making requests (1)

Which two of these requests for help sound more formal? Which are polite?

1 Can you give me a hand, please?
2 Would you mind helping me?
3 Could you help me out please?
4 Would you be able to assist me?

2b. Phrases – making requests (2)

Complete these requests for help by unscrambling the letters in bold.

Excuse me, can you help me? ...

1 ... I've **tsol ym pstropas** and my flight leaves in two hours.
2 ... I think I've **speut ym clgueaole** from Canada. He won't answer my emails.
3 ... I've tried to **lseoc wond shti grapomr** but my laptop isn't responding.

2c. Phrases – offering a solution

Match these responses to the requests in 2b.

a   I can talk to him and smooth things over, if you want. _____
b   Do you want me to get our IT people to look at it? _____
c   I can find the phone number of the embassy, if you like. _____

2d. Phrases – offering to help

Sometimes people offer help 'spontaneously' (naturally, without planning). For each question, decide which of the three responses (a, b or c) to spontaneous offers of help is NOT appropriate.

1 *Can I give you a hand with the projector?*
   a Why?
   b No, that's fine. I think it's under control.
   c Oh thanks. I'm having some problems.

2 *Would you like me to take a picture of you?*
   a No, that's OK. But thanks for the offer.
   b Why would I want a picture of myself?
   c That would be great. Press this button here.

3 *Do you want me to call you a taxi?*
   a Yes, if you would please.
   b Thanks but I've already booked one.
   c I can do that myself, thank you.

4 *Shall I ask about tickets for tomorrow?*
   a Yes please, that would be very helpful.
   b No. I have internet access.
   c No thanks, I've decided not to go.

3. Speaking – solving problems

Look again at the situations in exercise 1. How would you request and offer help, using what you've learnt in exercises 2a–d?

4a. Listening – making recommendations (1)

17 Brad is talking to Ingrid about his trip to Europe. What does he ask about? Number the topics in the order they are mentioned.

a something to do as a tourist _____   c a souvenir for his parents _____

b a hotel _____   d a restaurant to take a business contact _____

4b. Listening – making recommendations (2)

17 Listen again. What does Ingrid recommend for each of the topics and why? Make notes.

a something to do as a tourist: _____

b a hotel: _____

c a souvenir for his parents: _____

d a restaurant to take a business contact: _____

4c. Phrases – recommendations

Use the words to write out Brad's requests and Ingrid's recommendations. Listen again to check.

1 a Can / recommend / reasonably priced one? *Can you recommend a reasonably priced one?*
  b suggest / book / room / Novotel.

2 a What / think / should do?
  b should take / bus tour.

3 a What / typical souvenir / Berlin?
  b If / were you / would get / something / Ampelmann Shop / Potsdamer Platz.

5. Phrases – when you can't help

Match the requests (1–4) to the responses (a–d) and then to the suggestions of who might help (i–iv). Draw lines to connect the three sentences.

1 My computer's crashed. Can you look at it?

2 Any thoughts on what wine we should order?

3 Can you get me tickets for the film festival?

4 Which is the best gallery to visit in Paris?

a I'm sorry, I can't. But I think it's easy to book online.

b I don't know anything about Macs, sorry.

c I'm afraid I'm not a connoisseur.

d I'm probably not the best person to ask about art.

i Ask Angie. She's the expert on painters and that sort of thing.

ii Marc might know. He's over there on the next table.

iii I'll ask my secretary to do it. What do you want to go and see?

iv I'll give Ingrid a call. She uses them for her design work.

6. Speaking – making recommendations

Work with a partner. Student A: ask student B for recommendations. Student B: if you know the answer, offer to help. If you do not know, apologize and suggest someone who might be able to help.

7. Social planner

Now turn to page 106 and add helping and recommending language to the social planner.

Module 3 Unit 4
Opinions, agreeing and disagreeing

In this unit you will look at:

- which topics to give your opinion about
- giving opinions
- agreeing and disagreeing
- positive and negative opinions
- being tactful
- exchanging opinions

1. Speaking – opinion topics

In general conversation, what topics would you be prepared to give your opinion about? Classify the following topics into *yes*, *no* or *it depends* (used when you cannot give a definite answer).

the weather	a type of art or music	someone you both know
the traffic	a sportsman or team	a new law
a political situation	a business problem	the state of the economy
a religious controversy	the environment	the board of directors

Discuss your choices with a partner. Explain the reasons for your choices.

For more vocabulary on some of the topics, see Module 9.

2a. Listening – giving opinions (1)

18 Listen to Marc and Angie. What are they discussing? Why does Angie want to talk about this subject?

2b. Listening – giving opinions (2)

18 Listen again. Decide whether Marc's opinion on these topics is positive or negative.

1 the economic consequences of the EU
2 the recent expansion of the EU
3 the EU now compared to its initial vision
4 the future of the EU in business

For practice on facts vs. opinions, see Module 6 Unit 2.

2c. Phrases – opinions, agreeing and disagreeing

Some of the following phrases are in the wrong category. Rearrange them under the correct headings.

Asking for opinions	Giving opinions	Agreeing and disagreeing
What do you think about …?	I'm sorry, I can't agree.	I see what you mean, but …
I don't agree.	Do you think …?	Absolutely.
Yes, that's right.	From my point of view, …	I'm sure that …
I think …	What's your opinion on …?	I'm convinced that …
In my opinion, …	It seems to me that …	How do you see it?
I agree with you.	I completely agree.	I'm sorry, but surely that's not right.

18 Listen again to Angie and Marc. Which of the phrases do they use in their conversation?

> **Pronunciation tip** When you disagree with someone it is important to emphasize the negative word in the sentence. *I'm afraid I **don't** agree with you*. It is the same if you use *but* to make a contrast: *I see what you mean **but** I think the Euro is a good idea.*
>
> 19 Listen to these sentences and try to repeat them. Can you get the emphasis right?

3. Vocabulary – giving a positive or negative opinion

Put these phrases into the correct position on the scale.

What do you think about …?

+

I think it's: _____ idea.

a bad	a very good	a poor
a brilliant	a good	an interesting
a terrible	quite an interesting	

–

Cultural tip ✓ You may not always agree with another person's opinion. Although direct disagreement is respected in many countries, in others you should be 'tactful' – careful in the way you speak and behave – when you disagree. What about your country? Do people disagree directly or are they tactful?

4. Phrases – being tactful

For each opinion, label one response A (agreement), one TD (tactful disagreement) and one DD (direct disagreement).

1 *I reckon the summers are getting warmer every year, you know.*
   a That's right. I've noticed that as well. _____
   b Of course not! You shouldn't believe everything you read in the papers. _____
   c I'm afraid I don't agree. I haven't noticed any change. _____

2 *In my opinion, the cut in interest rates won't help to boost investment.*
   a To be honest, I'm not sure that's right. It just needs time. _____
   b No no, that's wrong. You don't understand the economics. _____
   c How true. It's the wrong decision, in my opinion. _____

3 *I think these new laws will have a negative impact on our business.*
   a Absolutely! It's going to be a big problem. _____
   b I see what you mean, but I don't think it'll be as bad as you think. _____
   c You can't be serious! They're going to give us a huge boost. _____

5. Speaking – exchanging opinions

For this exercise you need a coin. Work with a partner. Look at the list of topics in exercise 1 of this unit.

Vocabulary tip ✓ The two sides of a coin are called 'heads' and 'tails'. How do you remember which side is which? The 'heads' side has a head on it.

Student A: ask student B for an opinion on one of the topics. Student B: toss the coin. If the coin comes up 'heads', agree with the opinion and add some more information. If it is 'tails', disagree and say why. When you are finished, student A should choose another topic from the list and start again.

6. Social planner

Now turn to the social planner on page 106 for more practice with opinions language.

Module 4 Unit 1
Going out for a drink

In this unit you will look at:

- places to go for a drink
- things to do in a bar
- offering to buy a drink
- declining a drink
- toasts
- describing drinks

1a. Vocabulary – places to go for a drink

a Label the pictures with the correct term: *coffee shop*, *pub* and *bar*.

1  2  3

b Which words in the box would you use to describe each place?

> noisy   crowded   sophisticated   smoky   traditional   quiet   trendy   busy   cosy   relaxed

1b. Speaking – where to go?

Which of the four places in 1a would you prefer to go to for a drink and to:

- talk with a customer or client?
- watch a sports event on TV?
- hear music?
- talk with a colleague?

Use the words from 1a (part b) to explain your choices. Compare your answer with a partner.

2a. Listening – going out for a drink (1)

🔘 20 Brad and Ingrid have just left the office after a long meeting. Where do they decide to go? Why?

2b. Listening – going out for a drink (2)

🔘 20 Listen again. Are these statements true or false? If they are false, what is the correct information?

1 Brad wants to go somewhere with music.
2 Brad likes the British pub they go into.
3 They sit at the bar.
4 Ingrid learnt about beer from an ex-boyfriend.
5 Ingrid does not drink alcohol.
6 They decide not to buy anything to eat.

2c. Vocabulary – things to do in a bar

Complete the verbs with the missing letters. Listen to the conversation again if necessary.

1 l _ _ _ _ _ to some music
2 h _ _ _ a chat
3 s _ _ at the bar
4 f _ _ _ a table
5 o _ _ _ _ a drink
6 g _ _ some nibbles

2d. Phrases – declining a drink

Do you remember why Ingrid ordered a coffee? Match the responses (a–c) to the offers of a drink (1–3).

1 What would you like?
2 Would you like a glass of wine?
3 One more before you go?

a No thanks, I don't drink.
b Not for me. I've had enough, thanks.
c An orange juice is fine for me, thanks.

🔘 21 Listen to the mini-dialogues to check your answers. Try to repeat the pronunciation.

2e. Speaking – decline politely

How can you respond to an offer of an alcoholic drink if:

- you have to go to a meeting in half an hour?
- you have to drive back to your office?
- you don't like what is being offered?
- you are on medication and shouldn't drink?

Work with a partner. Take it in turns to offer and decline the drink in each of these situations.

> *Cultural tip* Customs for drinking alcohol vary around the world. There are rules about the reasons for drinking alcohol (for example a special celebration), what and how much to drink (for example a single glass of wine with lunch), and when and where not to drink (for example for religious reasons).

3. Quiz – toasts around the world

A toast is when people drink together and say something to express their good wishes. Match these toasts (1–6) to the country (a–f).

1 Prost	2 Gan Be	3 Cheers	4 Kampai	5 Santé	6 Salud
a Japan	b UK/USA	c China	d France	e Spain	f Germany

What do you say in your country?

> *Cultural tip* In some countries it is typical to buy a round of drinks in a bar or pub. In others, people do not often buy drinks for other people. What is considered typical where you come from? Do the same rules apply if you take someone to a place that does not serve alcohol, such as a coffee shop?

4a. Vocabulary – describing drinks

What do these words mean when used to describe drinks? Use your dictionary if necessary.

dry   sweet   fruity   malty   bitter   full-bodied

4b. Speaking – describe a drink

lager   cider   cranberry juice   gin   espresso   Guinness   tea   milkshake

Choose a drink from the box that you have had before. How would you describe it to someone who has never tried it? Use some of the words and phrases below, and from the rest of the unit:

It's made from … (*the main ingredient*)
It's quite / pretty / very / extremely … (*describe the taste*)
It's usually served … (at room temperature / chilled / over ice)
People sometimes mix it with … (*another drink*)

5. Speaking – roleplay

Work with a partner. Imagine you are in a hotel bar. Follow the conversation maps on page 80 (student A) and page 82 (student B). Try to use as many of the words and phrases from this unit as possible.

For more drinks vocabulary, see Module 2 Unit 3.

6. Social planner

Now turn to page 107 and fill in the social planner with your own drink preferences and customs.

Module 4 Unit 2
At a restaurant

In this unit you will look at:

- things on the dinner table
- questions and answers in a restaurant
- expressing preferences and complaints
- paying for your meal

1. Speaking – doing business in restaurants

When taking business associates to restaurants, how much of the time do you think should be spent talking business?

2. Vocabulary – the dinner table

Match the words to the pictures. There is one word you do not need.

plate   side plate
wine glass   water glass
knife   butter knife
fork   dessert spoon
soup spoon
soup bowl   cup
saucer   tea spoon
chopsticks   napkin

3a. Listening – in the restaurant (1)

22 Ashok has invited Brad out for dinner. Listen and choose the correct answer to these questions.

1 Where has Brad been to an Indian restaurant?
a in Boston
b in Los Angeles

2 What does Brad not eat?
a vegetables
b red meat

3 Why is there no beef on the menu?
a because Indian people don't like it
b because of religious rules in India

4 What does Ashok suggest they order?
a several local dishes
b the local speciality

3b. Listening – in the restaurant (2)

22 Ashok is the host and Brad is his guest. Listen again. Who asks each of these questions?

1 What do you fancy? __Host__
2 Have you tried Indian before? _____
3 What should I order? _____
4 Are you a vegetarian? _____
5 Do you like spicy food? _____
6 Is there a local speciality? _____

3c. Phrases – responses to food questions

Now match these possible responses to four of the questions in 3b. Write the question numbers.

a Not really. It upsets my stomach. _____
b Yes, I recommend the cassoulet. _____
c I'd like to try the seafood pasta. _____
d No, this is my first time. _____

For more on preferences, see Module 3 Unit 1. For making recommendations, see Module 3 Unit 3.

4a. Phrases – preferences and complaints

Look at the sentences 1–10 below. Label them either 'P' (personal preference / requirement) or 'C' (complaint).

1 My food is not very hot.
2 This steak is rare. I wanted it well done.
3 I can't use chopsticks. Could I have a fork, please?
4 I'm massively allergic to nuts.
5 I tried sushi once. I'm afraid I didn't like it.

6 I'm afraid I don't eat meat. I'm a vegetarian.
7 Excuse me, we've been waiting for an hour.
8 I'm sorry, but this soup is much too salty.
9 I'm really not very keen on shellfish.
10 These vegetables are undercooked.

Do you have any preferences or requirements when it comes to food or drink? How would you express these in English?

4b. Speaking – a complaint

When was the last time you had a problem in a restaurant? Did you have to complain? What did you do and how was the problem resolved? Compare your experience with a partner.

5a. Phrases – paying for your meal (1)

Match the words to the definitions.

1 split
2 go halves
3 bill
4 tip
5 check

a a piece of paper that shows how much money you owe after eating in a restaurant
b the American word for bill in a restaurant
c a small amount of money that you give to someone, in addition to what you owe
d to share something by dividing it into separate parts
e to share the cost of something with someone so that you each pay 50%

5b. Phrases – paying for your meal (2)

You have just had dinner with an important business associate. For each of the situations (1–2) choose which of the responses (a, b or c) is NOT appropriate.

1 *Shall we split the bill?*
   a No, you're my guest. I'll get this.
   b OK, let's go halves.
   c Only if you pay for those three bottles of champagne you drank.

2 *Should we leave a tip?*
   a No way! The service was lousy!
   b There's no need. The service is included.
   c Yes, about ten per cent on top of the check should be enough.

Cultural tip   In some countries, such as the United States, it is very common to leave a tip whether or not you have had good service. In others, people never leave a tip or the size of the tip depends on your opinion of the service you have received. What is the situation in your country?

6. Speaking – roleplay

Work with a partner. You are in a restaurant. It is lunchtime. Student A turn to page 80. You start the conversation. Student B turn to page 82. Use the prompts to roleplay the situation. Don't forget to use some of the phrases from Brad and Ashok's conversation in exercise 3.

For more food vocabulary, see Module 2 Unit 3.

7. Social planner

Now turn to page 107 and fill in the social planner with information about restaurant language and local specialities.

Module 4 Unit 3
At a conference

In this unit you will look at:

- words associated with conferences
- talking about the conference programme
- things you collect at trade fairs
- making contacts
- questions and answers at conferences
- planning which events to attend

1. Conferences and trade fairs

Look at the pictures. At which event are you most likely to:

- see a demonstration of a new product?
- buy a book?
- exchange business cards with someone?
- meet new contacts?
- hear a presentation about a new idea?
- arrange meetings?
- collect free product samples?

trade fair

conference

2a. Vocabulary – conference words

All of these words are associated with conferences. Match each one to their definition.

1	name badge	a	a lecture or presentation about a subject
2	keynote speech	b	a document that tells you what will happen at an event
3	talk	c	the main presentation at a conference or formal event
4	workshop	d	a large room or building used for meetings and lectures
5	programme	e	an occasion when people meet to discuss and learn about a subject
6	auditorium	f	an object used to identify you that fastens onto your clothes

2b. Listening – the conference programme (1)

🔘 **23** **Claire and Ashok have completed the registration and are discussing the conference programme. Listen to their conversation. What is the main subject of the conference? Who is giving the main talk on the subject?**

2c. Listening – the conference programme (2)

🔘 **23** **Take a look at the conference programme on page 83. Then listen again to Claire and Ashok and decide whether these statements are true (T) or false (F).**

1 Ashok has forgotten to put his badge on.
2 Claire has seen John Barrymore give a talk.
3 Claire thinks Eunice May is a good speaker.
4 Ashok decides against the blended learning talk.
5 They both want to go to Jeremy Small's workshop.
6 They are late for the keynote speech.

3a. Vocabulary – things you collect at trade fairs

Companies at trade fairs usually distribute materials to potential customers and clients. Which of the words in the box are printed materials to advertise a product or service, and which are other types of promotional materials? Write them in the correct categories in the table on the next page.

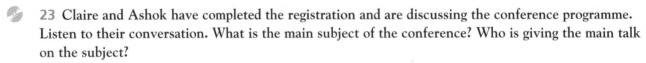

giveaway   freebie   brochure   sample   leaflet   tester   flyer   handout

Printed materials	Other types of material

3b. Speaking – publicity materials

Look again at the materials in 3a. Tick (✔) any that your company produces. Discuss your answers.

4a. Vocabulary – making contacts

Ashok attends Diana Phillips' presentation about online learning. After the presentation he waits to talk to her. Put the lines of their conversation into the correct order.

a Ashok: That was a very interesting presentation. I really learnt a lot. __*1*__

b Diana: Thank you. I'm glad you found it useful. Do you use online training? _____

c Diana: Certainly. Do you have any plans for lunch? _____

d Ashok: It's not very common in my country yet. _____

e Diana: Thank you very much, Mr Patel. Here's mine. _____

f Ashok: Mumbai, in India. Let me give you my card. _____

g Diana: Where are you from? _____

h Ashok: Thanks. I would be interested in talking about this some more if you have time. _____

For more on introductions, see Module 1 Unit 4.

4b. Speaking – making contacts

Look again at the conference programme on page 83. Imagine you have attended one of the presentations or workshops. Work with a partner and use Ashok and Diana's conversation from exercise 4a as an example. Introduce yourself to the speaker and arrange to meet for lunch.

5. Phrases – at the end of the conference

Claire meets Ashok at the end of the conference. Reorganize these words to make questions.

1 Have / good / you / a / time / had ?

2 Have / anything / you / useful / learnt ?

3 What / interesting / was / the / session / most ?

4 Did / you / any / contacts / make / useful ?

5 Are / going / again / you / year / next ?

What answers might you give to these questions?

6a. Speaking – conference planner

Look again at the conference programme and 'conference planner' on page 83. Then complete the conference planner with the events that you would like to attend. Divide up the sessions between you and your partner.

6b. Speaking – the end of the conference

Work with the same partner as in exercise 6a. You have now come to the end of the conference and want to compare notes. Roleplay a conversation between the two of you, telling each other about the events you have been to. Use new language from this unit to develop your conversation.

7. Social planner

Turn to the social planner on page 107 and prepare notes for your next conference.

Module 4 Unit 4
Meeting and greeting visitors

In this unit you will look at:

- different types of visitors
- what to say when arriving at reception
- meeting and greeting visitors
- being on time or late
- making excuses
- first conversations

1. Visitors

These people are all visitors. Where do you think are they visiting and why? Discuss your ideas.

2. Phrases – arriving at reception

Brad has just arrived at Ashok's office. Use the verbs in the box to complete the conversation.

> take   see   help   sign   let   have   call   put

Receptionist: Good morning sir. Can I ¹_____ you?
Brad: Good morning. Yes. I'm here to ²_____ Mr A J Patel. My name's Brad Ruby.
Receptionist: Just a moment, let me check. You ³_____ an appointment at 10 o'clock, is that right?
Brad: Yes, that's right.
Receptionist: Could you ⁴_____ in here please Mr Ruby, and ⁵_____ on this visitor's badge. I'll ⁶_____ Mr Patel's secretary and ⁷_____ her know you've arrived.
Brad: Thank you very much.
Receptionist: Would you like to ⁸_____ a seat; Mr Patel will be down in a moment.
Brad: Thanks.

3a. Listening – meeting and greeting visitors

24 Listen first to Ashok greeting Brad, then to Claire greeting Ingrid. Choose the correct options.

1 Brad is visiting Ashok's home / office.
2 Brad asks for a glass of water / a cup of tea.
3 Ashok's new offices are more modern / closer to his clients.
4 Ingrid gives Claire a bottle of wine / a box of chocolates.
5 Claire invites Ingrid into the kitchen / the sitting room.
6 Claire offers Ingrid a glass of white wine / French wine.

3b. Phrases – meeting and greeting visitors

24 Listen again. Write the phrases (a–j) in the correct usage category (1–5) on the next page.

a ~~Can I get you something to drink?~~
b Make yourself comfortable.
c Come in.
d He's on his way.
e Come and sit down.
f She'll be here soon.
g Would you like a drink?
h You can put your bag over there.
i Let me take your coat.
j Come through.

1 Inviting the visitor to enter:	2 Dealing with the visitor's clothing or luggage:	3 Offering the visitor a seat:	4 Offering the visitor refreshments: *a*	5 Saying another visitor is not here yet:

4a. Vocabulary – being on time or late

Fill in the gaps with *on time, in time, late* or *too late*.

1 I always like to be _____ for meetings.

2 Sorry I'm _____ . Have I missed anything?

3 I'm afraid you're _____ . The train has gone.

4 We arrived just _____ for the presentation.

4b. Phrases – excuses

Which of these are acceptable excuses for not arriving on time? *Sorry to keep you waiting ...*

1 ... I got stuck in traffic.

2 ... I couldn't follow your useless map.

3 ... my watch has stopped working.

4 ... we had an urgent problem at the office.

5 ... the taxi driver didn't know the way here.

6 ... I couldn't find a place to park.

7 ... my wife didn't wake me up in time.

8 ... my flight got in late.

4c. Speaking – making excuses

Write down as many excuses for being late as you can think of. After 60 seconds, stop and compare your ideas with a partner. Which excuse is the most common? Which is the most extraordinary?

Cultural tip   Perceptions of being 'on time' and 'late' can vary. If you are attending a meeting or a social event in another country, find out what the local view is.

5. Speaking – meeting, greeting and first conversations

Look at the maze below, showing a dialogue between a host and their visitor. Reorder the words in bold to make questions. Then, work with a partner: one of you is the host and the other the visitor. Use the questions (host), answers (visitor) and directions (in *italics*) in the maze to roleplay the dialogue.

Question 1: was journey How your?
It was very good. (*go to question 3*) / It was terrible. (*go to question 2*)

Question 2: dear, that was why Oh?
My flight/train was delayed/cancelled. / The traffic was terrible. / My car broke down/was stolen. (*go to question 3*)

Question 3: first Is your time here this?
Yes it is. (*go to question 5*) / No, it isn't. (*go to question 4*)

Question 4: here When you before were?
I was here for a meeting/for a holiday/to see a friend. / I often come here. / I used to live here. (*go to question 5*)

Question 5: How staying you long are?
I'm flying home tonight. (*go to question 7*) / Until tomorrow. / For the rest of the week. (*go to question 6*)

Question 6: are staying you Where?
At the Holiday Inn/the Hotel Royale/my brother's flat. (*go to question 7*)

Question 7: are where things you How are?
Things are great/pretty good/not bad/difficult at the moment. (*continue the conversation until the other visitors arrive*)

6. Social planner

Now turn to page 107 and fill in the social planner with your own personal visitor information.

Module 5 Unit 1
Describing, comparing and talking about the best

In this unit, you will review:

- the use of adjectives to describe people, places and things • the language of comparison • the language of superlatives

> **!** **Communication breakdown!**
>
> 'What's London like?' 'Yes – I like London.' 'I'm sorry – I don't understand.'
>
> **Why is there a communication problem here? Turn to page 99 to check your answer.**

1. Find the grammar mistake

Read the sentences. Six of them contain a classic grammar mistake in the use of adjectives, comparatives or superlatives. Find the mistakes and correct them. Then check your answers on page 99.

1 Madrid is the same than Barcelona.
2 It is the most beautiful city of the world.
3 She is the nicest woman I know.
4 It's a car blue.

5 The economical situation is very bad.
6 It is more beautiful than any other painting.
7 This question is more easy than that one.
8 This is the worstest company in the world.

2. Grammar focus – adjectives, comparatives and superlatives

Was exercise 1 difficult? If so, study the grammar focus table on page 94 to clarify this language area.

3a. Vocabulary – adjectives

How would you describe these people, places and things? Use the adjectives in the box.

1  2   3  4   5  6

handsome   historic   light   portable   automatic   dark-haired   pretty   busy   peaceful   fast   green   blond

3b. Practice – adjectives and opposites (1)

Write down the opposites of the following adjectives. The first letter is given for each one.

1 modern – a_____   2 beautiful – u_____   3 hard working – l_____   4 quiet – n_____

> *Learning tip*   It sometimes helps to learn words along with their opposites. Note that many adjectives use prefixes like *-in*, *-un* or *-im* to form the opposite.

3c. Practice – adjectives and opposites (2)

Add prefixes to make the opposites of these adjectives. Use the prefixes *-in*, *-un* or *-im*.

1 ____accurate   3 ____sympathetic   5 ____patient
2 ____reliable   4 ____wise   6 ____tolerant

Grammar tip ✔ Remember that in English, the adjective comes **before** the noun. For example: *We have had a year successful* (incorrect); *We have had a successful year* (correct). This is a very common mistake amongst English learners because in many other languages the adjective comes second. The same is true for comparative and superlative adjectives in English: always before the noun.

4. Speaking – describing places, people and things

'What's your office like?'   'What's your boss like?'   'What's your best-selling product like?'

Choose one of the three questions and describe the place, person or thing to a partner. Then change roles. Continue until you have answered all three questions.

5a. Listening – comparing favourite cities

25 **Listen to Angie and Marc. Which cities do they mention? And in what order? Put the correct number next to the cities that are mentioned, and an 'X' next to any that aren't.**

New York City ___   Berlin ___   Paris ___   London ___   Tokyo ___   Barcelona ___

5b. Practice – comparative and superlative forms

Write the comparative and superlative forms of these words. Use the grammar focus table if necessary.

1 slim   2 trendy   3 cheap   4 effective   5 good   6 bad

5c. Practice – comparative sentences

Write comparative sentences using the prompts below. The first one has been done for you.

1 (New York / much / exciting / anywhere else) *New York is much more exciting than anywhere else.*
2 (London / so much / busy / Paris)
3 (London / crowded / most capital cities)
4 (London / dirty / most capital cities)
5 (It / much / expensive / most other places)
6 (Paris / romantic / anywhere else I know)

25 **When you have finished, listen again to Angie and Marc's conversation to check your answers.**

6. Writing & speaking – comparing two things

Choose one (or more) of the following pairs and write three sentences comparing them.

Apple Mac / PC   working in the office / working at home
sports car / family car   driving to work / taking the train

Compare your sentences with your partner. What do you agree on? What do you disagree on?

7. Writing & speaking – the best …

Write down your answer to three of the following questions, then discuss with a partner.

What's the best …

… way to learn a language?   … way to motivate staff?   … project you've ever been involved with?
… mobile phone?   … corporate website?   … hotel you've stayed at?

8. Social planner

Now turn to the social planner on page 108 for more practice in this area.

Module 5 Unit 2
Talking about the present and using modals

In this unit, you will review:

- the present simple and present continuous tenses
- the use of modal verbs

Communication breakdown!

'Who do you work for?' 'I'm working for IBM.' 'So – why are you leaving?' 'I'm sorry. I don't understand.'

What has gone wrong? Check page 99 to compare your answer.

1. **Find the grammar mistake**

   Read the eight sentences. Six of them contain a classic grammar mistake in the use of present tenses. Find the mistakes and correct them. Then check your answers on page 99.

   1 I am work for Metro.
   2 I'm working now.
   3 He like Rome.
   4 I'm usually going there by underground.
   5 I work rarely at this factory.
   6 I'm not understanding your accent.
   7 Do you work abroad much these days?
   8 Your boss wants to join us?

2. **Grammar focus – present tenses**

   Was exercise 1 difficult? If so, study the grammar focus table on page 94 to clarify this language area.

   Grammar tip | Some verbs are not usually used in the present continuous, eg *believe, can, feel, know, like, love, need, prefer, understand, want, wish.*

3. **Practice – using present tenses**

   Choose the best option for each sentence.
   1 I <u>stay / am staying</u> at the Grand for a few days.
   2 We <u>work / are working</u> on the project.
   3 <u>Do / Does</u> the driver know how to get there?
   4 I <u>work / am working</u> for them for two months.
   5 He <u>like / likes</u> the sound of the new project.
   6 <u>I'm usually going / I usually go</u> there by taxi.
   7 <u>Do / Does</u> you know Jenny, the sales manager?
   8 <u>Is / Does</u> your boss work in that office?

4. **Writing & speaking – your current work and projects**

   Use these sentence beginnings to describe your current work and projects, using the correct tense:

   I usually …   I never …   Now, I'm …
   At the moment, I'm …   I often …   I sometimes …

   _____
   _____
   _____
   _____
   _____
   _____

   Tell your partner about your job. Then change roles.

Communication breakdown!

'When is your flight? I'll book your taxi.' 'I mustn't leave before four o'clock.' 'I'm sorry – I don't understand.'

What has gone wrong? Check page 100 to compare your answer.

5. Find the grammar mistake

Read the eight sentences. Each of them contains a classic grammar mistake in the use of modal verbs. Find the mistakes and correct them. Then check your answers on page 100.

1 I cannot to speak German.
2 We must to go now.
3 I don't can understand you.
4 He don't have to work at night.

5 We mustn't pay VAT – it's optional.
6 You shouldn't to smoke.
7 You mustn't pay by cash, you can pay by credit card.
8 Have you to work every day?

6. Grammar focus – modal verbs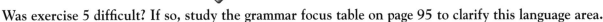

Was exercise 5 difficult? If so, study the grammar focus table on page 95 to clarify this language area.

7. Practice – using modal verbs

Choose the best option in each question.

1 You <u>must / mustn't</u> send the contract as soon as it's ready.
2 We <u>don't have / can</u> to hire a data projector – we already have one.
3 I <u>can't to / can't</u> speak German.
4 We <u>must / don't must</u> go now.
5 I <u>don't can / cannot</u> understand this decision.
6 He <u>don't have to / doesn't have to</u> work at night.
7 Our company is so small that we <u>don't have to / mustn't</u> pay VAT.
8 You <u>shouldn't / may to</u> smoke in here.

8a. Writing – rules and regulations

You are the CEO of a new company and you need to create a set of rules and regulations for the employees to follow. Write six sentences and use at least four different modal verbs. Topics to consider: dress code, overtime, time to start/finish, etc. Use the example to help you get started.

> You should start work at 8am Monday to Thursday, and 9am on Fridays.
> _____
> _____
> _____
> _____

8b. Speaking – decision time

Discuss your proposed rules for the new company with a partner. Try to justify your choices and agree on five rules to take forward. Remember to use the language of giving opinions, agreeing and disagreeing from Module 3 Unit 4.

9. Social planner

Now turn to the social planner on page 108 for more practice in this area.

Module 5 Unit 3
Talking about the past

In this unit, you will review:

- the past simple tense
- the present perfect tense

Communication breakdown!

'How long are you here for?' 'For three minutes.' 'Oh, I thought you would be here until Friday.'

What's the problem? Turn to page 100 to find out if you are right.

1. Find the grammar mistake

Read the eight sentences. Seven of them contain a classic grammar mistake in the use of the past simple or the present perfect. Find the mistakes and correct them. Then check your answers on page 100.

1 I'm living here for three years.
2 I've lived here three years ago.
3 I didn't finish the report yet.
4 I saw my boss last night.
5 I have lived here since three years.
6 I have spoken to Ashok yesterday.
7 I am here since Friday.
8 I've gone to Rhodes six times.

2. Grammar focus – past simple and present perfect

Was exercise 1 difficult? If so, study the grammar focus table on page 95 to clarify this language area.

Pronunciation tip   Regular verbs ending in -ed have one of three different sounds: /ɪd/, /t/ and /d/:

- /ɪd/: Verbs ending with a /t/ and /d/ sound in the infinitive add an /ɪd/ sound in the past: eg want-wanted, need-needed
- /t/: Verbs ending with unvoiced sounds such as /p/, /k/, /f/, /s/, /ʃ/ and /tʃ/ in the infinitive add a /t/ sound in the past: eg watch-watched, pass-passed
- /d/: Other verbs add a /d/ sound in the past: eg play-played, seem-seemed

 26 Listen to these words and try to repeat them.

3a. Practice – past simple forms

Put the underlined verbs into the past simple.

1 Why is your English so good? I <u>live</u> in New Jersey for two years.
2 What did you use to do? I <u>design</u> websites. Oh yes, and I <u>work</u> for a publisher.
3 When <u>do you start</u>? I <u>join</u> the company in 2006.
4 Where did you study? I <u>go</u> to UCLA for a while, but then I <u>drop out</u> of university.
5 What did you do after university? I <u>get</u> a job in London but I <u>don't like</u> living there.

Networking tip   When we meet someone, we often tell them things that we did or used to do, or funny or entertaining stories. It is usual to use the past simple for this.

3b. Practice – past simple in stories

Put the lines of this story into the correct order.

a However, as I left the police station, I dropped my passport. _____
b So, I went to report the theft to the police. _____
c You'll never believe what happened to me when I first went to Paris. __*1*__

d Luckily, someone picked it up and gave it back to me. Can you believe it! _____

  e My bag was stolen from the Eurostar. _____

  f When the train arrived at the Gare du Nord it had gone, and all I had left was my passport. _____

4a. Practice – past participle forms

The past participle is the form of the verb that we put with the subject and 'have' to make the present perfect. Put the following verbs into the past participle. Be careful! Some of them are irregular.

send   receive   write   talk   be   take   read   try   leave   live   arrive   come

> **Grammar tip** ✔ When we meet people, we often ask them about their experiences, using the present perfect and the word 'ever'. For example: *Have you ever eaten squid?* It is also common to use the present perfect when first answering these questions, but we usually change to the past or present simple when giving further details. For example: *No, I haven't. I don't like seafood.*

4b. Phrases – past experiences

Match the questions (1–4) to the answers (a–d).

1 Have you ever been to India?

2 Have you seen the latest Bond movie?

3 Have you read any Murakami?

4 Have you tried sukiyaki?

a Not yet, but I like Daniel Craig.

b Yes. He's my favourite Japanese writer.

c Yes. Once, when I was in Nagoya.

d Yes, a couple of years ago. I went with my wife.

5a. Practice – time markers

Choose the best option in the sentences below. Use the grammar focus table to help you if necessary.

1 Our customer relations department has been based in India <u>since / for</u> last year.

2 I was in Spain on business <u>since four days / four days ago</u>.

3 I've been very happy here <u>up to now / last year</u>.

4 We haven't met the new sales executive <u>already / yet</u>.

5b. Revision – past simple or present perfect?

For each question below write the verb in brackets in the correct form: past simple or present perfect. Remember to look at the rest of the sentence for clues on which tense is needed.

1 I _____ (work) in the USA three years ago.

2 _____ you ever _____ (attend) one of those seminars?

3 In 2009 I _____ (get) promoted to regional marketing manager.

4 She _____ (finish) the report already.

5 The CEO _____ (not make) any mistakes so far.

6. Writing & speaking – hot topics

Write about one of the following 'hot topics'. Remember to use the past simple and present perfect correctly, and to get the right verb forms.

- Something funny that happened to me

- A nightmare business trip

- What I've done in the last year

- My working life so far

Work with a partner and tell them about your description or story. If you are listening, ask questions to get more information or if anything isn't clear.

7. Social planner

Now turn to the social planner on page 108 for more practice in this area.

Module 5 Unit 4
Talking about the future and speculating

In this unit, you will review:

- future forms
- conditional types 0, 1 and 2

Communication breakdown!

'What are you doing tomorrow?' 'I will go to Paris. I will take the Eurostar. Then I will have a meeting. Then I will come home.' 'Er … OK.'

What's the problem? Turn to page 100 to find out if you are right.

1. **Find the grammar mistake**

   Read the six sentences. Three of them contain a classic grammar mistake in the use of the future. Find the mistakes and correct them. Then check your answers on page 100.

   1 I present at a conference next month.
   2 I'm flying next Saturday.
   3 We leave at 6.00, according to the itinerary.
   4 I do it now.
   5 I think United are winning the cup next season.
   6 I'm going to start up my new business this year.

2. **Grammar focus – future forms**

   Was exercise 1 difficult? If so, study the grammar focus table on page 96 to clarify this language area.

3a. **Practice – future uses**

   Look again at the correct versions of sentences 1–6 in exercise 1. Label the future forms according to their use: PI (plan/intention), PR (prediction), ID (instant decision), FA (fixed arrangement) or ST (schedule/timetable). Use the notes in the grammar focus table to help you.

3b. **Practice – future forms**

   Going to, will, present continuous or present simple? Write the verbs in brackets in the correct future form. Clue: there are two examples of each future form in the exercise.

   Example: I *'m going to take* (take) her on my next business trip to Malaysia.

   1 I think we _____ (get) a good bonus this year.
   2 I think I _____ (learn) a new language next year.
   3 I _____ (not repeat) the same mistakes with the next project.
   4 I _____ (meet) my wife at 6.
   5 My train _____ (leave) in a couple of minutes.
   6 I _____ (let) you know when I'm next in town.

3c. **Writing & speaking – ten minutes with the future**

   You have two minutes to answer each question using the relevant future form.

   1 Write down one prediction for the years: 2020, 2050, 2100.
   2 Write down three fixed arrangements that you have for next week.
   3 Write down three plans or intentions that you have for the future.
   4 Write down three schedules or timetables relevant to you this week.
   5 It's dark; it's cold; you're tired. Write down three instant responses to help.

Communication breakdown!

'What would you do if you lost your job?' 'Lost my job? But I didn't lose my job.'

What's the problem? Turn to page 100 to find out if you are right.

4. Find the grammar mistake

Read the three sentences. Each of them contains a classic grammar mistake in the use of conditionals. Find the mistakes and correct them. Then check your answers on page 100.

1 When shares are cheap, we'd buy a lot of them.
2 If we sell our shares, we'd lose a lot of money!
3 If we sold our shares, we'll lose millions.

5. Grammar focus – conditionals

Was exercise 4 difficult? If so, study the grammar focus table on page 96 to clarify this language area.

 Pronunciation tip   It can be difficult to catch contractions like *'ll, 'm, 've, 't, 's* and *'d*. See Module 6 Unit 4 for more on this.

6a. Practice – conditionals (1)

Which situation is more likely to happen? Label each sentence 'A' (always), 'P' (possible) or 'I' (improbable). Then complete sentences 4a and 4b in your own words.

1 a If the credit crunch ends, we'll be laughing.
  b If the credit crunch ended, we'd be laughing.

2 a If we go left, we'll get to London.
  b If we went right, we'd hit the sea.

3 a If we lose a contract, we're disappointed.
  b If we lost a contract, we'd be disappointed.

4 a If they give me a pay rise, …
  b If they gave me a pay rise, …

6b. Practice – conditionals (2)

Look at these conditional sentences and write the verbs in brackets in the correct form. Use the grammar focus table to help you if necessary.

1 If I _____ (have) a lot of money, I would make a film.
2 If we _____ (not hurry), we'll miss the train.
3 When there _____ (be) a lot of traffic, I get to work late.
4 If I _____ (not have) to work, I probably wouldn't.
5 Which country _____ (you choose) if you could live anywhere?
6 If there was another recession tomorrow, we _____ (be) in real trouble.

7. Writing – what would you do if …?

Write down three answers to one of the following questions.

What would you do if …

… you had to cut costs in your company?
… you were the prime minister of your country?
… you had to give 20 per cent of your company's profits to charity?

8. Social planner

Now turn to the social planner on page 108 for more practice in this area.

Module 6 Unit 1
Being a good listener

In this unit, you will look at:

- reasons why listening is difficult
- listening for gist
- listening for specific information
- strategies to improve listening
- checking information
- active listening

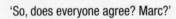

'So, does everyone agree? Marc?'

'Um, I'm sorry. I didn't understand.'

1a. Why is listening so difficult?

Think about your answer to this question. Make a list of reasons why listening is so difficult.

- *Speaker talking too quickly …*

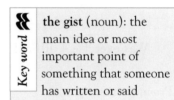

Key word

the gist (noun): the main idea or most important point of something that someone has written or said

1b. Listening – for gist

27 Listen to the six mini-dialogues. Write down the order in which you hear the problems.

Contractions ___   Accent ___   Idioms ___   Slang ___   Speed _1_   Vocabulary ___

1c. Listening – for specific information

27 Listen again and answer the questions below.

Dialogue 1: What date does the first speaker want to meet?
Dialogue 2: What specialist word is used by the first speaker?
Dialogue 3: What idiom does the first speaker use?
Dialogue 4: Where is the first speaker from?
Dialogue 5: What slang expression does the first speaker use?
Dialogue 6: Can you write the contraction that the first speaker uses? 'I _____ done that.'

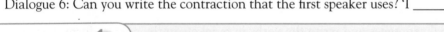

Pronunciation tip   Sounds change in 'connected speech' (everyday conversation). Sometimes a sound disappears completely. For more on this, see Module 6 Unit 4.

2a. Strategies to improve listening

Read the eight student learning strategies for improving listening. Tick any that you use.

I watch DVDs of films I know at the same time as reading the subtitles.
I watch the news on TV. The pictures give me clues.
Before a presentation, I write down some words that I think the presenter will use.
I listen to podcasts about subjects I'm interested in.
I listen to the BBC news for five minutes on the radio every day.
I try and have conversations with native English speakers.

☐
☐
☐
☐
☐
☐

2b. Speaking – discuss strategies

Compare your answers with a partner. How effective do you think these strategies are? Can you add any more useful activities to improve listening?

3a. Listening – checking information

 28 Listen to two extracts from a meeting. Who is the better listener: John or Sandra? Why?

 Networking tip 〉 When someone is speaking quickly, you can repeat something back to them to check and clarify what they have said.

3b. Phrases – checking information

Put the words in the correct order to make checking questions.

1 a / slower? / Could / little / you / say / that   2 please? / Could / that / you / repeat

For more on checking and clarifying, see Module 7 Unit 4.

4a. Active listening

 29 Listen to these three dialogues. Circle who you think is the best listener and the worst listener.

Best: Listener 1 / Listener 2 / Listener 3   Worst: Listener 1 / Listener 2 / Listener 3

4b. Writing – what is an active listener?

Describe an 'active listener' in your own words. Turn to page 100 to compare your answer.

> *An active listener ...*

5a. Quiz – are you a good listener?

Are you a good listener? Complete the quiz. Then check your score on page 100.

> ## Are you a good listener?
>
> ***Circle the relevant number for each question.***
>
> **1** I try and give the speaker my full and undivided attention. 0 1 2 3 4
> **2** If I don't understand what the speaker says, I ask them to repeat. 0 1 2 3 4
> **3** If someone speaks too quickly, I ask them to slow down. 0 1 2 3 4
> **4** I research the subject before attending a presentation. 0 1 2 3 4
> **5** I listen actively by smiling and nodding. 0 1 2 3 4
> **6** I ask questions to obtain more information. 0 1 2 3 4
>
> **Key:**
> 4=always
> 3=usually
> 2=sometimes
> 1=rarely
> 0=never
>
> Total score: ____

5b. Speaking – action plan

Compare your answers to the quiz with a partner. Discuss an 'action plan' on how to improve your listening. Make sure to include some of the strategies from exercises 2a and 2b.

6. Social planner

Now turn to the social planner on page 109 and write in your action plan.

Module 6 Unit 2
Listening for the general idea

In this unit you will look at strategies for listening and:

- vocabulary associated with the economy
- answering general questions about a conversation
- identifying opinions, facts, causes and effects
- summarizing a conversation

1. The credit crunch

Do you remember the credit crunch (the period from 2008 to 2009 when it was very difficult to borrow money from banks)? Read these statements. Do any of them describe your experience of that time?

'It was a difficult time – the banks didn't want to lend any money.'

'It was terrible for us – the bottom fell out of our business.'

'We did really well. In fact, our company grew in size.'

2. Vocabulary – economic problems

Match the words to the definitions.

1 stock exchange   a money from the government to help prevent companies from going bankrupt
2 property prices   b the current cost of houses and other types of buildings
3 rescue package   c when a company or person has no money and cannot pay what they owe
4 go bankrupt   d a place where people buy and sell shares in companies
5 recession   e a period when trade is not successful and there is a lot of unemployment

3. Listening for the general idea

30 Getting the general idea of a conversation is more important than catching every word. Marc, Claire, Angie and Ashok are having lunch together during a conference. Listen to part of their conversation.

4. General questions

30 Listen to the conversation and answer the questions.

1 What are they talking about?
2 Why are they discussing this topic?
3 Who is angry about the report? Why?
4 Who had to make people redundant?
5 Which two people work in banking?
6 Who benefited from the situation? Why?

5. Opinions vs. facts

It is important to be clear about whether someone is expressing their opinion or stating a true fact. Look at these statements. Label each one either 'O' (if the person is expressing an opinion) or 'F' (if they are stating a fact).

1 Marc: In my opinion it didn't consider the human cost. ___
2 Angie: I think it did have some positive results. ___
3 Marc: Clients cancelled projects with my company. ___
4 Claire: In 2009 all those international rescue packages were agreed. ___
5 Ashok: My company doubled in size during the first half of 2009. ___

6. Cause and effect

It can sometimes be difficult to follow a conversation because the connections between events and actions are not clear. Match the effects (1–5) to the causes (a–e).

Effects (changes produced):

1 People working in banking thought that the good times would go on forever because …
2 Marc had to lay off hundreds of workers because …
3 Claire is optimistic about the future because …
4 Companies in Europe and America starting sourcing their IT services from India because …
5 Ashok's company doubled in size in the first half of 2009 because …

Causes (the reasons for changes):

a … her company is recruiting new staff.
b … clients all over the world cancelled projects with his company.
c … the value of the stock exchange and property had been going up for years.
d … he got lots of new clients from Europe and America.
e … they needed to cut costs.

7a. Summarizing (1)

A good test of how well you have understood a conversation is how well you can summarize it. For this, we often use 'reported speech'.

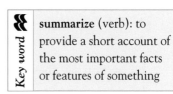

Key word

summarize (verb): to provide a short account of the most important facts or features of something

Grammar tip

When we change from direct to reported speech the verb changes forms.

For example: Marc: 'It'<u>s</u> an interesting time.' (present simple) … *becomes* … Marc said it <u>was</u> an interesting time. (past simple)

Because most of the story about the credit crunch is in the past simple, the reported speech form uses the past perfect. This is *had* + the past participle of the verb. For example: Angie: 'It <u>was</u> all over the newspapers last week.' … *becomes* … Angie told us that it <u>had been</u> all over the newspapers the previous week.

Note also how *last week* changes to *the previous week*. Other time words which change in reported speech are *next* (which becomes 'the following'), *now* (which becomes *then*) and *today* (which becomes *that day*).

Complete the reported sentences by putting the verb into the correct form.

1 Claire: 'It was a horrible period.'
   Claire said it __*had*__ __*been*__ a horrible period.

2 Marc: 'All over the world, clients cancelled projects.'
   Marc told us that all over the world, clients _____ _____ projects.

3 Claire: 'I'm definitely optimistic.'
   Claire said she _____ definitely optimistic.

4 Claire: 'Ashok, what was your experience of the credit crunch?'
   Claire asked Ashok what his experience of the credit crunch _____ _____ .

5 Ashok: 'My company doubled in size.'
   Ashok said his company _____ _____ in size.

7b. Summarizing (2)

Now it is your turn to summarize the conversation. Listen one last time to the conversation and make notes. Then, work with a partner and compare your summaries, using reported speech as you talk through them. Did you or your partner catch any information the other did not?

There is a wide range of further listening practice throughout this book. Look for any exercises with 'Listening' in the title. For more on discussions at conferences, see Module 4 Unit 3.

8. Social planner

Now turn to the social planner on page 109 for an extra task to develop your listening skills.

Module 6 Unit 3
Listening for specific information

In this unit you will look at:

- saying email addresses
- listening for names and contact details
- giving and updating contact details
- listening to and understanding technical facts and figures
- describing items
- giving and receiving directions

1a. Vocabulary – saying email addresses

a Match the email symbols (1–4) to the way they are said (a–d).

1	@	3	_	a	underscore	c	dot
2	.	4	-	b	dash/hyphen	d	at

1 @   3 _
2 .   4 -

a underscore   c dot
b dash/hyphen   d at

b Can you say these email addresses?

i marc.gisset@central-international.fr   **ii** aj_patel@iol.tech.co.in   **iii** bj.ruby@greatbear-productions.com

How do you say your email address?

Pronunciation tip   In order to avoid mistakes when spelling names a good technique is to use words that begin with the letters you are saying or checking. Some people use the names of famous towns. For example: *A for Amsterdam. Is that B for Berlin?*

1b. Listening – names and contact details (1)

31 Claire and Ashok have recently met each other while at a conference. Listen to part of their conversation and correct these statements.

1 Claire has left all her business cards in her hotel room.
2 The information on Claire's business cards is out of date because she changed her job.
3 Claire writes her new contact details on her old card.
4 Claire also gives Ashok her home phone number.

> **Windman Brothers Bank**
> Claire Thanet
> Director of Human Resources
>
> 12–18 Jamaica Street
> London SW1 8UH
> United Kingdom
>
> Tel: 020 477 4730
> Mobile (work): 0788 078 3792
> Email: cthanet.hr@windmanbros.co.uk

1c. Listening – names and contact details (2)

31 Listen again to Claire and Ashok, and correct the information on Claire's business card above.

1d. Speaking – updating contact details

Work with a partner. Your business cards are out of date – take it in turns to ask for and give the updated information. For the cards and new information, turn to pages 80–81 (student A) and page 83 (student B).

1e. Writing – updating contact details

Choose one of the business cards from 1d. Write an email to send to your contacts with the updated information. Details of the cards can be found on pages 80–81 and 83.

For more on introductions, see Module 1 Unit 4.

2a. Listening – technical facts and figures

32 Listen to Brad, Angie and Marc and put these numbers into the specification table: *3, 3G, 12, 30, 3.5, 150.*

Apple iPhone	¹ Weight: about _____ grams	² Screen: _____-inch touch-sensitive	³ Network: _____
	⁴ Movie formats: _____	⁵ Email attachment formats: _____	⁶ Camera: _____ megapixels

2b. Speaking – describing an item or place

Choose one of these items/places and prepare a short description similar to Brad's.

- Your mobile phone   - Your laptop computer   - Your car   - Your office

Work with a partner. Take it in turns to give your descriptions.

3a. Listening – giving and receiving directions

33 Listen to Claire and Angie giving Ingrid directions. Mark the location of the restaurant on the map.

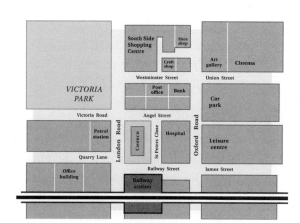

3b. Listening – summarizing

How would you summarize the route from the office building to the restaurant? Make notes.

34 Then listen to Ingrid's summary and compare it with yours.

3c. Vocabulary – directions

Look at this description, giving directions to a hotel. Complete the gaps with words from the box.

miss	in front of	out	side	follow	straight	turn	next	on	with
turning	corner	end	behind						

Go ¹_____ of this building, ²_____ left, then walk all the way to the ³_____ of the street and turn right. Go down there for a few hundred metres, then take the third ⁴_____ on the right, which is called Cannon Street. You can't ⁵_____ it – it's a really busy road. There is a garage on the right ⁶_____ of Cannon Street and just ⁷_____ that is a narrow street. You should go down this street and ⁸_____ it until you see a vegetable shop on the ⁹_____ . Then go ¹⁰_____ on past the vegetable shop and just ¹¹_____ that is an arcade. The hotel is ¹²_____ to the arcade, ¹³_____ the right side of the street. Is that clear? Are you ¹⁴_____ me?

3d. Writing & speaking – giving directions

How would you give directions from your place of work/study to:

1 the nearest railway station?   2 the nearest bank?   3 the nearest (good) restaurant?

Use words and phrases from 3c to help you. Write out the directions, then explain them to a partner.

4. Social planner

Now turn to the social planner on page 109 and make notes to help you with spelling and directions.

Module 6 Unit 4
Listening: pronunciation

In this unit you will focus on the different aspects of pronunciation:

1 Individual sounds) (2 Word stress) (3 Intonation) (4 Contractions) (5 Weak forms) (6 Sounds in connected speech) (7 Accents

1a. Pronunciation – definitions

Match the words and phrases (1–7) in the speech bubbles above to the explanations (a–g) below.

a People from different countries or parts of a country speak in different ways. _7_

b All of the specific phonetic sounds in English, like /p/ and /b/. ___

c When we speak quickly, words can get joined together, and a new sound is created. ___

d We often combine two words (I will) to make one (I'll). ___

e In a word with two syllables, one syllable is stressed – so it sounds stronger than the other syllable. ___

f This 'pattern' refers to whether your voice goes up or down when you speak. ___

g The phonetic symbol for this is /ə/. A word like 'a' can be said in a strong way, or a weak way. ___

1b. Individual sounds

 35 **Listen to mini-dialogues 1–4. Match each dialogue to the correct area of the phonetic chart to the right. Then listen again and repeat each line after you hear it. Use the pause button if you need to.**

Click each symbol to hear it spoken.

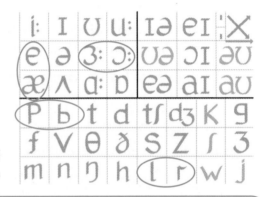

MACMILLAN

Copyright of Macmillan 2008

Learning tip ✓   Do you know which English sounds cause you problems? You can visit the Macmillan website (www.macmillanenglish.com) and download an interactive version of the phonetic chart, which can help you identify any problem areas with individual sounds.

2. Word stress

 36 **Here are some words which can cause communication problems. <u>Underline</u> the stress and listen to check.**

advertisement	photography	development	agenda
plenary	interesting	product	misunderstanding
record (noun)	record (verb)	transfer (noun)	transfer (verb)

3. Intonation

 37 **Up or down? Mark the intonation pattern on these questions, as in the example. Turn to page 101 to check your answers, then listen and repeat the questions with the correct intonation.**

<u>Example:</u> What's your name?

1 Where are you from?

2 I wonder if you can help me?

3 Excuse me, could you tell me how to get to the bus station?

4 What time does the next session begin?

4. Contractions

 38 Listen to the three sentences and decide if you hear sentence a or b each time.

1 **a** What will happen to them?   2 **a** I haven't met her.   3 **a** I am so tired.
   b What'll happen to them?   **b** I've not met her.   **b** I'm so tired.

Then check your answers on page 101 and practise saying the 'b' sentences.

> *Pronunciation tip*   Did you know that contracting can help you sound less direct? Study these two offers, and read the reactions of the listener in brackets.
> - I'll help you. (Oh, how nice!)   - I will help you. (OK, OK. I didn't say you couldn't help me!)

5. Weak forms

 39 Did you know that the most common sound in English is /ə/? This symbol – called the 'schwa' – represents the 'weak form'. Every vowel in English can be said with the schwa. Some common words can be pronounced with both strong and weak forms. Listen and repeat the strong and weak forms of these words:

   and   of   you   me   she   does   have   must

 40 Now listen to the three sentences and decide if the <u>underlined</u> words are strong or weak.

1 <u>Can</u> you help me?   2 You <u>should</u> stay.   3 It's <u>a</u> boy!

6. Connected speech

41 In each of the four extracts, you will hear two individual words, and then the same two words together in a sentence. How do the words change when they are put together? Complete the table.

Extract	First word	Second word	How do they sound together?
1			
2			
3			
4			

Compare your answers with the explanations on page 101. Then listen to the words and sentences again and try to repeat them. Try to sound as natural as possible.

7. Accents

Listen to three different groups of English speakers, both native and non-native. Write the number of the speaker next to the country. Consider what is different about the accents. Can you imitate them?

42 Group 1:	**43** Group 2:	**44** Group 3:
Native English speakers	Non-native English speakers	The United Kingdom
Australia _____ Canada _____	Mexico _____ Finland _____	Wales _____ Ireland _____
Caribbean _____	India _____ Japan _____	England-Liverpool _____
South Africa _____ USA _____	Russia _____	England-London _____ Scotland _____

See Module 7 Unit 4 for more on checking and clarifying.

8. Social planner

Now turn to the social planner on page 109 and make notes on your own pronunciation problems.

Module 7 Unit 1
Making small talk

In this unit you will look at:

- why small talk is difficult
- opening questions
- starting small talk
- finding a common topic
- question tags
- connecting events in a story

1. What makes small talk difficult?

What difficulties do you have with small talk? Tick the statements that are true for you.

- I don't have the words to talk about topics. ___
- I often don't know much about the topics. ___
- It is difficult to find a common topic. ___
- Small talk is different in different countries. ___

2a. Opening questions

Which of these questions do you think are NOT appropriate for starting a small talk conversation?

1   Is this your first time in California?
2   Have you lost weight?
3   Did you see the match yesterday?
4   I like your scarf. Where did you get it?
5   Are you here for the conference?
6   I like your watch, how much did that cost?
7   Is that the new Nokia? Is it good?
8   What are the men like in your country?
9   Are you supposed to be here?
10 Why did you leave your last company?

2b. Speaking – starting a small talk conversation

Choose a person from the left column and a situation from the right column. How would you start a conversation? Choose a question from exercise 2a or suggest your own.

A colleague from another country	On a plane	At a conference
A visitor from another company	Before a meeting	After a meeting
A senior manager in your company	During a coffee break	At a restaurant

Work with a partner. Start the conversation and see how it develops.

For more on language at conferences, see Module 4 Unit 3. For restaurants, see Module 4 Unit 2.

3a. Listening – finding a common topic (1)

45 Listen to Claire and Brad. Which topics do they mention? Which is of common interest?

1   the weather in Turkey
2   the shops at Heathrow Airport
3   why Brad's flight was delayed
4   the books of Orhan Pamuk
5   Brad's new bag
6   a murder in the news

3b. Listening – finding a common topic (2)

45 Listen again. Choose the correct ending to these sentences.

1   Brad bought a book at the airport because:
   a his flight was delayed and he had a long wait.   **b** he is very interested in Turkish literature.
2   Brad has:
   a read the book and enjoyed the story.   **b** started to read the book and likes the style.
3   Claire recommends another novel to Brad because she thinks:
   a he would enjoy the story more.   **b** the one he is currently reading is too easy.
4   Brad is going to read the book Claire recommends:
   a now.   **b** after he has finished his current book.

4a. Listening – question tags

45 To involve the other person more, some people make questions by adding a 'tag' to a statement. Listen again and add the tag to each question below.

Claire: They have so many shops there, [1]_____?

Brad: The story's quite slow, [2]_____?

4b. Grammar – question tags

> *Grammar tip* ✔
>
> Question tags are formed using the negative of the verb 'be' (as in Brad's question above) or the auxiliary, for example *will*, *have*, *did* or *do* (as in Claire's question). The tense of the verb in the question tag has to be the same as the tense of the verb in the main sentence. For example: You *know* Angie Wong-Smith, *don't you*? (present simple)/ The conference *was* smaller last year, *wasn't it*? (past simple)
>
> **For more on the grammar of the present, past and future, see Module 5.**

Add tags to these statements to turn them into questions.

1 China is a huge country, _____?

2 You're staying all week, _____?

3 The weather has improved, _____?

4 Angie is from Hong Kong, _____?

5 They start next year, _____?

6 It'll be good to see them, _____?

5a. Vocabulary – connecting events in a story

Use the words in the box to link the parts of Angie's story below.

but	at first	when	so	then	suddenly

Angie: That reminds me of the time I met Fidel Castro. I was staying at a hotel in New York. [1]_____ I came down for breakfast one morning there were dozens of security people and journalists standing near the door. [2]_____ I thought I could avoid them [3]_____ then the group moved and blocked the way to the restaurant. [4]_____, there he was in front of me.

Brad: Who? Fidel Castro?

Angie: Yes. He said good morning – in Spanish – and I answered. [5]_____, before I could say anything else he invited me to have breakfast with him.

Brad: Wow! What did you do?

Angie: I hesitated before saying I had to meet my husband. [6]_____ we both said our goodbyes and I never saw him again.

> *Vocabulary tip* ✔
>
> The following words and phrases are useful when you are describing a sequence of events:
> *first of all … secondly … thirdly … and finally …*

5b. Speaking – a short story

Choose one of the topics below and prepare a short story about it that you could tell to a colleague or business associate. Remember to use connecting words like those in exercise 5a.

- My first job
- The first time I spoke English in a meeting
- The time I met someone famous
- An exciting sporting event I remember

Work with a partner. Tell each other your stories, using the conversation in 5a as a model.

6. Social planner

Now turn to the social planner on page 110 for more small talk practice.

Module 7 Unit 2
Active listening

In this unit you will look at:

- what 'active listening' means
- listening and showing interest
- follow-up questions
- 'Have you ever …?' questions

1. Active listening

'Active listening' means saying and showing that you are interested in what the other person is telling you. Which of these techniques would demonstrate that you are actively listening?

1 Asking more questions about the subject
2 Changing the topic to something more interesting
3 Nodding your head
4 Maintaining eye contact with the other person
5 Using your mobile phone to send a text message
6 Laughing when you hear something funny

For more on body language, see Module 8 Unit 2.

2a. Listening – showing interest

 46 Listen to Marc telling Claire about a hospital experience. Which of the responses below does Claire use to show she is listening and interested in Marc's story?

Oh yes?   That's a shame   Uh-huh?   That's good news   How awful   That was lucky   That's funny
No!?!   Really?   That's incredible!   Is that so?   That's great   Right   Oh dear   Go on   I see

2b. Phrases – showing interest (1)

Write down all of the phrases in 2a which show that:

1 you are interested and want someone to continue
2 you are impressed or think something is amazing
3 you think something is fortunate
4 you think something is unfortunate

2c. Phrases – showing interest (2)

What response would you make to these comments? Choose a phrase from 2a for each one. Note: There may be more than one possible answer.

1 So, we've won a new contract in Poland. _____
2 In the end nobody noticed that it was the wrong version of the report. _____
3 That reminds me of the first time I had to present to the board of directors. _____
4 I broke my leg while I was on a skiing holiday. _____
5 Did you know that there are no Starbucks cafes in Italy? _____

3a. Listening – follow-up questions

 46 Claire asks Marc short questions to show she is following his story and to push the conversation forward. Listen again and complete the four questions she asks.

1 What _____ ?
2 What _____ ?
3 What _____ ?
4 What _____ ?

3b. Practice – follow-up questions (1)

Complete Ashok and Ingrid's conversation with suitable question words.

Ashok: Have you been on holiday this year?
Ingrid: Yes, although it seems like a long time ago.

Ashok: [1]_____ was it?

Ingrid: Back in February.

Ashok: [2]_____ did you do?

Ingrid: We went snowboarding.

Ashok: Really? [3]_____ did you go?

Ingrid: We usually go to Switzerland but we went to Italy this year.

Ashok: Oh yes? [4]_____ was that?

Ingrid: Because it's a lot cheaper and there's more snow. Have you ever been snowboarding?

3c. Practice – follow-up questions (2)

Ashok's follow-up questions in 3b are in the past, as the conversation is about a previous holiday.

a Change Ashok's questions to ask about a routine. Use the adverb *usually* where possible.	b Now use 'going to' to change the questions so that they ask about future plans.
1 _____ ?	1 _____ ?
2 _____ ?	2 _____ ?
3 _____ ?	3 _____ ?
4 _____ ?	4 _____ ?

For more on adverbs of frequency, see Module 2 Unit 1. For the future, see Module 5 Unit 4.

3d. Speaking – ask and answer

What did you do for your last holiday? What are your plans for your next holiday? Using Ashok and Ingrid's conversation as a model, work with a partner to ask and answer the questions.

For more on talking about travel, see Module 2 Unit 1.

4a. 'Have you ever …?' questions

Grammar tip There are three basic answers to 'Have you ever …?' questions: *Yes, I have*, *No, I haven't* and *No, not yet* ('yet' indicates that the person has some intention of doing this in the future).

Look at the small talk extracts. First, complete the questions with the correct form of the verb in brackets. Then, complete the answers with one of these phrases: *Yes, I have; No, I haven't; No, not yet.*

1 Ashok: Have you ever _____ (try) Indian food?
   Brad: _____ . But I don't think it was very authentic.

2 Claire: Have you ever _____ (be) to Edinburgh?
   Marc: _____ . In fact, I've never been to Scotland.

3 Angie: Have you ever _____ (work) with people from China?
   Ingrid: _____ . But I'm going to Shanghai in the spring to make some contacts.

4b. Speaking – 'Have you ever …?'

With a partner, ask and answer the questions in 4a. Then think of another ten 'Have you ever …?' questions. Then change partners and ask and answer the new questions.

For more on 'Have you ever …?' questions and past forms, see Module 5 Unit 3.

5. Social planner

Now turn to the social planner on page 110 for more work on active listening.

Module 7 Unit 3
Managing a conversation

In this unit you will look at:

- how to manage different types of conversation
- interrupting and dealing with interruptions
- bringing someone into the conversation
- changing the subject

1.   How would you manage?

What would you say in each of these situations? Compare your ideas with a partner.

- One person keeps talking and nobody else can speak
- Someone interrupts you when you are talking
- Someone says something you disagree with
- You want to talk about something else

2a. Listening – a three-way conversation (1)

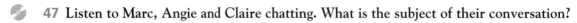 **47 Listen to Marc, Angie and Claire chatting. What is the subject of their conversation?**

2b. Listening – a three-way conversation (2)

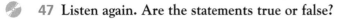 **47 Listen again. Are the statements true or false?**

1 Marc thinks French food is the best in the world.
2 Claire agrees with Marc about French food.
3 Angie has experience of different national cuisines.
4 French food is Angie's favourite.
5 Claire likes Chinese food because she lived in Hong Kong.
6 Claire says Chinese food is better than French.
7 Angie thinks they should all agree about this topic.
8 Claire wants to change the subject.

3.   Phrases – interrupting

a In the conversation about food, Claire interrupts Marc and, later, Marc tries to interrupt Angie. Why would you interrupt someone during a conversation?

b Look at the phrases 1–10 below. Which of them would you use to:

a interrupt and make a comment?
b interrupt and ask for an explanation?
c interrupt and agree?
d interrupt and disagree?

e allow someone to interrupt you?
f prevent someone from interrupting you?
g ask someone to go on after your interruption?

1 Sorry to interrupt, but I'm afraid I don't agree.
2 Can I say something quickly?
3 Sorry to interrupt, but …
4 Go ahead.
5 Sorry to interrupt, but I think [Angie] is right.

6 Could I add something here?
7 Please continue.
8 Just a moment, let me finish what I was saying.
9 Sorry, could I just say, …
10 Sorry to interrupt. Could you explain that?

Cultural tip     How people feel about interruptions depends on where they come from. Sometimes it is acceptable to stop a person because you want to speak and sometimes it is considered impolite.

For more on turn-taking, see Module 8 Unit 4.

4. Phrases – bringing someone into the conversation

Claire brought Angie into the conversation with Marc because she wanted her opinion on the topic. In these extracts, the words in *italics* are used to bring a third person into the conversation – but they are in the wrong order. Put the words into the correct order to make phrases.

1 Ingrid: It looks like the world economy is slowing down again.
 Ashok: I'm not sure, Ingrid. In fact, in India, the economy is booming. *you think what do*, Angie?
 Angie: I think you're both right. It depends on your point of view.

2 Brad: I find the politics of the European Union really confusing. How about you, Ashok?
 Ashok: Yes, me too. Claire, *know you this might.* When will the UK join the Euro?
 Claire: Oh dear. I don't really know. I doubt it'll be any time soon.

3 Marc: To tell you the truth Claire, I don't know the difference between PCs and Apple computers.
 Ingrid, *of experience this some have you* – can you explain?
 Ingrid: Well, I'm a designer. I've always used Apple myself.

5. Phrases – changing the subject

> **Grammar tip** ✔
>
> You can change the subject of a conversation in two ways:
> 1) <u>Directly</u>: when you clearly say you would prefer to talk about another topic – for example: *I don't think this is the right time to discuss politics. Ingrid, tell us about your trip to Australia.*
> 2) <u>Indirectly</u>: when the changing of the topic is less obvious – for example, you might use a pause in the conversation to change the subject. *That's interesting … So … have you seen that story in the newspaper about …?*

Look at the conversation excerpts 1–5 below, and decide if the person is changing the subject in a direct or indirect way. Write either 'D' (direct) or 'ID' (indirect).

1 Angie: Let's not talk business, this is a social occasion. Ashok, have you found a new flat yet? _____
2 Brad: That reminds me of something that happened to my colleague. _____
3 Claire: Let's talk about something else. How was your holiday, Marc? _____
4 Ingrid: Oh look, there's Brad. Come and tell us about your latest project. _____
5 Marc: I'm afraid I don't know very much about football. Do you like tennis? _____

6. Speaking – a three-way conversation

Look at the conversation map. Choose a topic from the list on page 81. In groups of three (student A, B and C) have a conversation using appropriate phrases from the unit. When you have finished, change to another topic on the list and go back to the start.

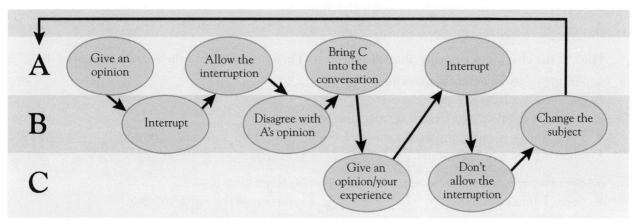

7. Social planner

Now turn to the social planner on page 110 and focus on the most useful phrases for you.

Module 7 Unit 4
Checking and clarifying

In this unit you will look at ways of:

- checking and clarifying
- rephrasing
- generalizing and giving examples
- ending a conversation

1. Sorry?

Can you think of a situation when you did not understand what someone was telling you? How did you deal with the situation? Did your actions help you to understand? Compare experiences with a partner.

2a. Listening – for gist

48 **Listen to Ashok talking to Marc and Ingrid. What are they talking about?**

2b. Listening – for detail

48 **Listen again and choose the correct answer to each question.**

1 Has Ingrid been to India?
   a No, but she would like to.   **b** Yes, and she found it very exotic.
2 Why does Marc think India and China are similar?
   a Because they are both in Asia.   **b** Because they are both big countries with expanding economies.
3 What is the population of India?
   a About 1,000,000,000,000.   **b** About 1,200,000,000.
4 According to Ashok, what is the main language of India?
   a Hindi.   **b** English.
5 Does everyone in India speak English?
   a Yes, but only as a second language.   **b** No, but it's important for businesspeople.

2c. Listening – checking and clarifying

48 **Listen again. Each of the three people has to check something that was said to them to make sure they understood correctly. Match the person to the piece of information they want to have clarified.**

1 Marc   **a** the use of English in India
2 Ashok   **b** the population of India
3 Ingrid   **c** a comparison of India with China

3. Phrases – checking and clarifying

Look at the checking/clarifying phrases a–j below. Then put them into the correct categories 1–5.

1 Asking someone to repeat something: _____
2 Showing you have not understood: _____
3 Asking someone to put something in a different way: _____
4 Repeating or summarizing what someone has said to check your understanding: _a,..._____
5 Showing you now understand: _____

a So, in other words, you're saying ...?
b Sorry, I didn't catch that.
c Could you explain what you mean?
d OK, I see what you mean.
e Sorry, I'm not with you.

f OK, that's clear now.
g Could you go through that again?
h Could you explain?
i So that's ...
j So, if I understand correctly, ...

Networking tip — Successful networking usually involves regular checking and clarifying to ensure that the conversation is progressing smoothly and there are no misunderstandings.

4. Phrases – rephrasing

'Rephrasing' involves saying the same thing with different words. Match the complicated explanations (1–3) to their rephrased versions (a–c). What phrases are used to introduce the rephrasing?

1 The build-up of greenhouse gases in the upper atmosphere combined with other diverse factors is causing an apparently exponential rise in global temperatures.	2 Australian varieties often use the same grapes and fermentation techniques as in France but factors such as the soil, amount of sun and storage have a significant impact on its bouquet.	3 We have an object-orientated system allowing you to input user variables to automatically write the HTML. A result is that you can make major savings in programming and coding.

'Sorry, I don't follow.'

a What I'm trying to say is that there are many reasons why the two wines have different tastes.	b In other words, our software offers a quick and cheap way of building websites.	c Let me put it another way: the planet is getting hotter every year due to environmental change.

5. Vocabulary – generalizing and giving examples

In small talk we often 'generalize' (make general statements) or provide examples, instead of giving detailed explanations. For each sentence below, use a word from the box to fill in the gaps.

on the whole	mostly	roughly	for instance	actually

1 _____ , did you know that India has the second biggest population in the world?
2 _____ , people in the construction industry are very pessimistic at the moment.
3 I like all kinds of music, but I _____ listen to artists from Asia these days.
4 I love to go to art auctions. Christie's in London, _____ .
5 I have _____ one weekend in three when I don't have to work or travel.

6. Phrases – ending a conversation

Reorganize the words in *italics* to make phrases suitable for ending a small talk conversation.

1 Claire: OK, *go got I've to*, Ashok. *talking been to it's nice you*.
   Ashok: Well, *for thanks chat the*. See you soon.

2 Ingrid: Look, it's nearly eleven o'clock. *start to it's meeting the time*.
   Angie: Oh yes, *business we down to get should*.

3 Marc: Well Brad, *you enjoyed to I've talking*.
   Brad: Me too Marc, *interesting thanks was it really*. I didn't realize we had so much in common.

See Module 1 Unit 4 for more on how to say goodbye.

7. Speaking – about a country

Work with a partner. Student A turn to page 81, student B turn to page 84. Take it in turns to tell each other about the country you have been given. Remember to use the language learned in the unit.

8. Social planner

Now turn to the social planner on page 110 and focus on the most useful phrases.

Module 8 Unit 1
Talking about your country: festivals and etiquette

In this unit, you will look at:

- country profiles
- collocations related to festivals
- talking about festivals and special dates
- international etiquette

> **Networking tip** ✔ Wherever you are networking you are likely to be asked about your country. Why not prepare a few things to say about it before your next networking event?

1a. Listening – talking about the UK (1)

 49 Listen to Claire talking about the UK. As you listen, number the topics in the order that you hear them (1–9).

The monarchy ___   Money ___   Multiculturalism ___
TV channels ___   The population ___   Famous singers and writers ___
Newspapers ___   Exports ___   Political parties ___

1b. Listening – talking about the UK (2)

49 Listen again and complete the missing information.

1 UK = four countries: _____, _____, _____ and _____
2 Exports: _____ goods
3 Currency: _____ pence makes one _____
4 The UK is very _____ diverse
5 Population: over _____
6 Three main political parties: the _____ , the _____ and the _____

2a. Note-making – country profile

Look again at the topics in exercise 1a. Make notes on these for ONE of the following:

- your own country   - a country you do business with   - another country you are familiar with

2b. Speaking & writing – country profile

Work in pairs and take it in turns to give information about your chosen country. If you are the listener, try to ask questions – you are a visitor from another country so there is a lot you need to know. If you are working on your own, write a short summary of your country.

3a. Vocabulary – festival collocations

Match the verbs (1–6) to the nouns (a–f) to create collocations for festival activities.

1 get together   4 give   a fireworks   d independence
2 set off   5 celebrate b forgiveness   e gifts
3 visit   6 ask for   c friends and family f for dinner

3b. Reading – festivals around the world

Match the different celebrations, festivals and holidays in the box to the descriptions 1–6 below.

Thanksgiving Day Christmas Day Chinese New Year Easter Ramadan New Year's Eve

1 'At this time of year we remember when Jesus came back to life. It's actually on a different date each year, over the weekend. We have hot cross buns on Good Friday.' _____

2 'We visit our family and friends – these are called, er, 'new-year visits'. We eat mooncakes. As usual, fireworks play a big part in the celebrations.' _____

3 'It's mainly celebrated in the USA and Canada, and the whole family gets together for a huge turkey dinner.' _____

4 'Traditionally, we give our gifts in the morning. I know in many other counties they do it the day before – on Christmas Eve, I mean.' _____

5 'We all wait around for midnight. It's different everywhere – here in Spain we eat twelve grapes as the bells chime. I think in London they set off lots of fireworks.' _____

6 'It falls in the ninth month of the Islamic calendar. Muslims around the world fast during the hours of daylight.' _____

3c. Note-making – a special date

Write down a special date in your own country. Why is this date important? What would you tell a visitor about this date? Add this date and some notes about it to your social planner.

4a. Reading – international etiquette

Knowing about local 'etiquette' (rules for behaving correctly in social situations) can make a big difference when networking internationally. Read the following tips from an international business etiquette guide. Can you guess which country each tip is about?

ETIQUETTE TIPS ACROSS CULTURES

1 **Tipping** Remember that you do not need to do this if the service charge is already included on the menu. If not, it is usual to give up to about 10% of the bill. Taxi drivers often expect a small one too.

2 **Exchanging gifts** This does not carry any negative meaning when doing business. If someone wishes to buy you a present they may ask what you would like – so don't be afraid to say what you would like! It is nice to show you appreciate the culture by asking for, say, an ink painting.

3 **Cuisine** Food is a great passion. Cooking involves careful preparation, attention to detail, and the use of fresh ingredients. When invited to someone's house, it is customary for the host or hostess to say 'Bon appetit' at the start of the meal.

4 **Business dress** Men should wear good quality suits. Ties are a must. Women should also wear suits, or conservative business dresses. It is strongly recommended that you do not wear anything flashy, such as obvious jewellery. This is linked with the egalitarian nature of life here and indeed elsewhere in Scandinavia.

5 **Exchanging business cards** Giving these to each other involves a degree of ceremony. Offer yours with both hands or just the right hand. You must treat any you receive with respect. If you are expecting to make a lot of contacts, it is a good idea to take a lot with you, preferably with one side translated.

4b. Writing & speaking – local etiquette tips

Make a local version of the article by writing five short etiquette tips for a country you know well. You can use any of the headings in the article and/or your own ideas.

If you are working in a group, share your tips with a partner. Did you use any of the same ones?

5. Social planner

Now turn to the social planner on page 111 and add information about your own country.

Module 8 Unit 2
Body language

Key word

body language
(noun): the movements
or positions of your body
that show other people
what you are thinking or
feeling

In this unit, you will look at:

- words to describe body language
- adjectives to describe 'state of mind'
- interpreting body language
- cultural differences in body language

1. Listening – what is body language?

50 **Listen to Claire giving an introduction to one of her workshops. As you listen, number the topic areas below in the order that you hear them. What does she say about each topic?**

Negative signals ___   Eye contact ___   Gestures ___
Non-verbal communication ___   Facial expressions ___   Misinterpretation ___

2a. Vocabulary – state of mind (the way you are feeling at the present time)

Match the state of mind adjectives (1–5) to their correct definitions (a–e).

1 defensive   a calm and not worried
2 nervous   b concentrating on a particular aim and not wasting time or energy on other things
3 engaged   c feeling excited and worried, or slightly afraid
4 relaxed   d showing you are angry or offended when you think that someone is criticizing you
5 focused   e involved in doing something

2b. Grammar – prepositions

Complete the sentences with one of the prepositions *about, on* or *in*.

1 I'm very nervous _____ the interview.
2 I was completed focused _____ her talk.
3 She was really engaged _____ the task.

4 There's no need to be so defensive _____ it.
5 I feel relaxed _____ the proposed changes.

3a. Interpreting body language

Match the interpretations of body language (a–f) to the people in the picture (1–6).

a This position may show that this person is defensive, although it may also just be comfortable. ___

b Open hands usually indicate someone who is very engaged in explaining something. ___

c This person may be thinking hard; people sometimes use both hands to cup their face in such cases. ___

d May be relaxed, or can be thinking hard. Hands behind the head, for example, is a sign of superiority. ___

e Playing with rings and jewellery, or hair, is often a sign of nervousness. ___

f Probably relaxed, although playing with coins, etc in a pocket may show nervousness. ___

Can you think of any other interpretations of the body language in the pictures?

3b. Our own body language

What messages do we send to other people through our own body language? Match the different types of body language (1–4) to the message being sent (a–d).

1	Leg moving up and down quickly	a	Defensive; alternatively, just comfortable
2	Doodling on paper during a meeting	b	Concentrating hard, resting or may even be falling asleep
3	Legs crossed	c	Concentrating? Or bored?
4	Eyes closed in a meeting	d	Probably nervous

> *Cultural tip* It is not always possible to know what other people's body language means. For example, avoiding eye contact may mean someone is shy, or that they are not interested in what you are saying, or simply that in their culture, people avoid eye contact.

3c. Writing & speaking – three types of body language

Prepare and present notes on three types of body language, including what they mean and how they can be misinterpreted. Try to use some of the new language from the unit.

4a. Cultural differences (1) – non-verbal communication

What is the situation with non-verbal communication in your culture? Put an 'X' in the relevant place on each line to show what is normal for you.

Touching other people: USUAL ⟵——————————⟶ UNUSUAL
Using hand gestures: USUAL ⟵——————————⟶ UNUSUAL
Maintaining eye contact: USUAL ⟵——————————⟶ UNUSUAL

4b. Cultural differences (2) – personal space

How close we stand to someone also varies in different cultures. Match the pictures to the descriptions.

a   These speakers are good colleagues and their proximity (or closeness) suggests they are quite intimate. Maybe they are gossiping or even sharing secrets. ___

b   These speakers are quite far apart, perhaps to show respect or to show a hierarchical relationship between them. ___

c   These speakers are, in terms of European culture, the 'correct' distance apart. ___

1

3

2

5. Speaking – states of mind before the meeting

Work in pairs. You are chatting with a colleague from another country before a meeting. Make small talk for three minutes. Make sure your body language shows your state of mind: for student A, this should be option 1 on page 81; for student B, option 1 on page 84. Afterwards, try to guess what each other's state of mind was. Then repeat the activity for state of mind options 2 and 3.

For more on making small talk, see Module 7 Unit 1.

6. Social planner

Now turn to page 111 and fill in your social planner with notes on key aspects of body language.

Module 8 Unit 3
Taboo areas and humour

In this unit, you will look at:

- taboo areas
- irony
- aspects of humour
- jokes

 taboo (noun): something that people do not do or talk about because it is very offensive or shocking

humour (noun): the quality that makes a situation or entertainment funny

Key word

1a. Taboo areas – subjects

Imagine you are networking. Which subjects can you talk about? Write the numbers of the topics in the box in the correct position on the arrow: safe, taboo, or somewhere in the middle.

1 sex   2 religion   3 politics   4 salaries   5 the weather   6 the economy   7 the news
8 a current war   9 a current business scandal   10 family   11 holidays   12 food

5
Safe ⬅——————————————————————➡ Taboo

1b. Speaking – safe or taboo?

Compare your answer to 1a with a partner and discuss your choices. Then check your answer on page 102. Do you agree with the answers given? Read the cultural tip below for more guidance.

Cultural tip It is not easy to define what a 'safe' or 'taboo' area is. For example, families may seem 'safe'. People may talk openly about divorce in one culture, but it may be taboo in another. A good socializer is sensitive to how individuals react to certain topics and will always stay away from potential taboo areas.

See Module 9 Unit 4 for ways to avoid talking about controversial subjects.

2. Humour and networking

Read the text below, which tells us a little more about the dangers of using humour in networking situations. Fill in the gaps with prepositions from the box. Each preposition may only be used once.

of   on   at   in   to   from

Humour is very different ¹_____ different cultures. People have individual tastes when it comes to humour. It is best ²_____ avoid jokes which make fun of groups ³_____ people. Sometimes, they laugh ⁴_____ other people's misfortune. Many people find these types of jokes offensive as different people have different senses of humour. It is best not to join in when such jokes are told. Stay away ⁵_____ telling any joke which is based ⁶_____ making fun of a set of people or a culture.

3a. Irony (1)

Read the dialogue and decide what the problem is. Then, check the answer in the cultural tip below.

(It's raining outside)
Speaker 1: 'Lovely day …'
Speaker 2: 'I don't understand.'

Cultural tip The problem here relates to 'irony'. Irony is a form of humour in which you use words to say the opposite of what they mean. Speaker 1 is being 'ironic': it is raining, so in reality it is not a lovely day at all. Irony is very common in British humour, but can be difficult to catch.

3b. Irony (2)

Read the four thoughts.

1 'I thought we began at 9.00.'

2 'I feel a bit cold.'

3 'I took a taxi but there was so much traffic.'

4 'This speech is going on forever.'

Now look at statements a–d. These are examples of 'gentle' ironic humour: they have exactly the same meaning as the thoughts above, but use opposite words. Match the ironic statements (a–d) to the thoughts (1–4).

a It would have been quicker to walk! ___

b I think my watch has stopped. ___

c It's the shortest talk I've ever heard. ___

d It's warmer outside! ___

3c. Speaking – irony across cultures

Is irony common in your culture? Do you have an example? Compare your answer with a partner.

4a. Listening – aspects of humour

51 Study the five words below. Listen to five dialogues in which people talk about different aspects of humour. Which of the five words is each dialogue about?

wisecrack ___   pun ___   in-joke ___   punch line ___   running gag ___

4b. Puns in business

'Puns' are often used in advertising. Many products are sold with a 'slogan' (a short phrase used to advertise something) which uses a play on words to make people remember it. For example:

1 'Taste. Not waist.' (slogan for Weight Watchers Frozen Meals – food to help people lose weight)

2 'Technology the world calls on.' (slogan for Northern Telecom – telecommunications company)

What is the pun in each of these examples? Check the answer on page 102.

5. Jokes – cartoons

Look at the two cartoons and decide how funny they are on a scale of 1–4 (1 = not funny, 2 = a bit funny, 3 = funny, 4 = very funny). Did you get the jokes? How similar or different is your sense of humour to others? Can you explain why you found the cartoons funny/not funny?

"Is anybody listening to me?"

6. Speaking – breaking the ice

You are meeting someone for the first time. Think of a funny story or joke which you could use to 'break the ice' (make them feel less shy or nervous). Remember to stay away from taboo areas!

Practise telling the joke to your partner.

For more on telling stories, see Module 7 Unit 1 and Module 5 Unit 3.

7. Social planner

Now turn to the social planner on page 111 and add notes about taboo areas and humour.

"If you hate being on hold and want to get on with your work, press 1 - if you want to be on hold for a long time so you can do the crossword, press 2."

Module 8 Unit 4
Attitudes to time and meetings across cultures

In this unit you will look at:

- different ways of working
- different attitudes to time
- meetings across cultures
- turn-taking

'Time runs differently for different people. In other words, our perceptions of time are very different.'
'If "time management" is difficult, remember: time always runs at exactly the same speed.
It is yourself that you have to manage!'

1. Speaking – about time

Do you agree or disagree with the two statements in the box?
Explain why.

Key word
multi (prefix): many, or several
linear (adjective): involving ideas or events that follow one after the other
task (noun): something that you have to do

2. Vocabulary – ways of working

Look at the key words in the box. Using these words, we can name two different types of worker: *multi-taskers* and *linear taskers*.

Now look at the diagrams below, which show two different ways of working. Write *multi-tasker* or *linear tasker* under each diagram. Which type of worker are you?

1 For some people, time is something which flows simultaneously on many different levels. For such people, it is easy to do several different things at the same time.

2 For some people, time runs forward in a straight line. These people usually complete one task before starting the next.

3a. Time and meetings

The meeting is scheduled for 10.00. In your culture, what time does this meeting actually start?

9.55   10.00   10.05   10.10   10.30   11.00

Have you ever worked in a culture where the answer to this question was different from yours? What happened? Compare your experience with a partner.

3b. Listening – Ashok's story

52 Listen to Ashok's story and answer the questions.

1 Where was he?
2 Why was he angry?
3 What did he do at 8.45?
4 Why did he suddenly feel relaxed?

3c. Speaking – cultural variations

Look at the two statements in the speech bubbles on the next page. Do you agree or disagree with these recommendations? How would you change them to match your own culture?

'Arrive 15 minutes early if it's a party.'

'Arrive at least 30 minutes late if the invitation is for dinner, and up to an hour late for a party or large gathering.'

See Module 4 Unit 4 for more on being late and on time.

4a. Turn-taking in meetings – the visitor

Have you ever attended a meeting abroad? Did people take turns to speak or did they all speak at the same time? Many businesspeople are surprised by the cultural differences in meetings, particularly when it comes to turn-taking. Look at the diagram showing different discussion styles across cultures. Match the visitor reactions (a–c) to the cultures in the diagram (1–3).

Culture 1	→ → → → → →	Long silences No interruption
Culture 2	→ → → → → → →	Short silences Some interruption
Culture 3	→ → → → → → →	No silences Constant interruption

a 'They're so quiet. Hardly anyone speaks at all!' ___
b 'They all talk at the same time! How can anyone actually hear what anyone else is saying?' ___
c 'They usually listen and wait until the speaker has finished before talking. They are so polite.' ___

4b. Turn-taking in meetings – the host

Match the following host comments (i–iii) to the correct parts of the diagram (1–3) in 4a.

i 'We communicate with each other.' ___
ii 'It's important to listen. It's impossible to hear the other person if you are talking at the same time.' ___
iii 'If someone asks a question, it is important to consider the answer. We value the concept of silence. It means you value what someone says.' ___

5a. Meeting expectations

Think about a future meeting in your company. Tick any features which you expect to happen.

I expect …

… to receive the agenda beforehand ☐   … to spend a long time socializing at the start ☐
… that the meeting will start on time ☐   … that everyone will be asked for their opinion ☐
… that there will be a chairperson ☐   … to finish by making an action plan ☐
… that people will use first names ☐   … that the meeting will finish late ☐

5b. Speaking – talking about meetings

Compare your answers to 5a with a partner. Discuss your own experiences of a meeting in a different culture. Was it as you expected, or different? How? Which do you think are the most important features on the list? Try to agree on an order (most important to least important).

6. Social planner

Now turn to page 111 and fill in your social planner with helpful notes on this topic.

Module 9 Unit 1
Talking about the arts

Key word

the arts (noun): activities such as art, music, film, theatre, and dance, considered together
genre (noun): a particular style used in cinema, writing, or art, which can be recognized by certain features

In this unit, you will practise talking about:

- music
- films
- art and paintings
- books

1a. Music genres

Match the groups, singers and composers (1–8) to the correct musical genre from the box.

| easy listening   pop   jazz   rock   folk   soul   classical   hip hop |

1 Bach / Mozart / Beethoven
2 Abba / Madonna / Coldplay
3 Miles Davis / John Coltrane / Ella Fitzgerald
4 Eminem / Public Enemy / Jay-Z
5 Metallica / The Who / Oasis
6 Frank Sinatra / Demis Roussos / Tony Bennett
7 Joan Baez / Gypsy Kings / Pete Seeger
8 Stevie Wonder / Aretha Franklin / Mary J Blige

Can you think of any more musical genres? Add them to the box.

Pronunciation tip   'Simon and Garfunkel live in concert.' The word 'live' here refers to playing music on stage, rather than in the studio. The pronunciation is /laɪv/. Don't get this confused with the verb 'to live' (pronounced /lɪv/) and the noun 'life' (pronounced /laɪf/).

 53 Listen to these three words and practise their pronunciation.

1b. Describing music

Match the words and phrases in the box to some of the groups, singers and genres in 1a.

| loud   relaxing   alternative   live   good to dance to   great lyrics   catchy   smooth   soothing   hard   melodic |

For more on talking about likes and dislikes, see Module 3 Unit 1.

2a. Film genres

 54 Listen to eight people talking about the kinds of films they like and write the number of each speaker (1–8) next to the correct genre.

animation ___   romantic comedies ___   musicals ___   sci-fi movies ___
war films ___   horror films ___   period dramas ___   action / thrillers ___

Vocabulary tip   We use the words 'dubbed' (changing the sound to the local language) and 'subtitled' (adding translation text to the bottom of the screen) when we talk about foreign-language films being shown in another country. What happens in your country? Which do you prefer?

2b. Describing films

Look at the adjectives in the box which can be used to describe different films. Think of one film you have seen which applies to each adjective.

| exciting   romantic   dramatic   thrilling   frightening   realistic   gripping   funny   fun |

3a. Art vocabulary

Look at the art vocabulary in the box, then write the words in the correct category below.

> oil   surrealist   watercolour   impressionist   canvas   brush   gallery   modern   classical   easel

Styles of art: _____

Words connected with painting: _____

3b. Listening – talking about art

1   2   3

 55 Listen to Angie and Marc talking about these paintings – which do they like and dislike? Which of these paintings do you like and dislike? Why? Compare with a partner.

See also Module 3 Unit 4 on giving opinions and agreeing and disagreeing.

4a. Book genres

Match the book genres on the left (1–6) to the titles on the right (a–f).

1 self-help   a *Murder on the Orient Express*
2 travel writing   b *Eric Clapton Now and Then*
3 cookery   c *A Handbook of Trees, Plants and Flowers*
4 gardening   d *The Five-Minute Chef*
5 biography / autobiography   e *The 7 Habits of Highly Successful People*
6 crime   f *Morocco on a Budget*

4b. Listening – about a book

56 Listen to Claire and Ingrid talking about books. Choose the correct answer for each question.

1 What is the title of the book Claire is reading? <u>Enduring Love / Amsterdam</u>
2 Who is the author? <u>Ian Rankin / Ian McEwan</u>
3 What does she think about the book? <u>She can't stop reading it. / She wants to put it down.</u>

5. Speaking – small talk about the arts

You are expected to make small talk about the arts at your boss's cocktail party. First, think of one example of each of the arts covered in this unit: music, film, art and books. Then prepare to say something about each one. When you are ready, roleplay the scene in groups of three or four.

Related units: Module 3 Unit 1, Module 3 Unit 4, Module 7 Unit 1 and Module 7 Unit 3.

6. Social planner

Now complete the social planner on page 112 with your own tastes and preferences in the arts.

Module 9 Unit 2
Talking about sport

In this unit, you will look at:

- finding a common interest in sport
- questions about sport
- sports vocabulary
- talking about sports
- talking about sports results
- sporting events

> **Networking tip** Some people think football is life. For others, it means nothing. A useful networking tip is to find out what you and the person you are talking to have 'in common' – in other words, what interests you share. If you are both interested in motor racing, great. However, if the other person finds cars boring, you should quickly move on to a different subject!

1a. Listening – finding a common interest in sport

57 Listen to the two dialogues between Marc and Ingrid, and Marc and Ashok. For each dialogue:

a What sports do the speakers talk about?   b Which sport do the speakers have in common?

1b. Phrases – questions about sport

Put the words in the correct order to make questions about sport.

1 see / Did / match / you / night? / the / last
2 sports? / you / Do / any / follow

3 will / cup? / think / Who / you / do / win / the
4 support? / you / do / Who

57 Listen to the dialogues again to check your answers.

2a. Vocabulary – sports (1)

Match the sports in the box to the pictures.

> sailing   athletics   rowing   basketball   weightlifting

1    2   3    4    5

_____   _____   _____   _____   _____

2b. Vocabulary – sports (2)

Identify the 'odd word out' in each line. Use the example to help you.

Example: ⟨marathon⟩/ triple jump / high jump / long jump (*marathon = running; others = jumping*)

1 pool / racket / stick / cue / bat
2 swimming / golf / canoeing / sailing

3 silver / gold / platinum / bronze
4 basketball / volleyball / netball / squash

3a. Listening – talking about sports

58 Listen to the eight people talking and write the correct speaker number next to each sport.

football __   rugby __   motor racing __   athletics __   tennis __   taekwondo __   golf __   swimming __

3b. Vocabulary – talking about results

Look at the sports 'headlines' (the most important stories) and fill in the gaps using words from the box.

> beat   won   lost   set   nil   points   wickets

1 Arsenal defeated

Once again Arsenal _____ their away leg. Bayern _____ by three goals to one.

2 Barça pip Real 1-0

After their one-_____ victory, the Catalans now top the table with 67 _____ .

3 Nadal-Murray thriller

Murray and Nadal were involved in a five-_____ thriller. The Spaniard finally won 6-2, 4-6, 7-6, 6-7, 9-7.

4 India win third test in Delhi

India took the last seven _____ to _____ England in a thrilling climax to the test series.

3c. Speaking – sport and you

Add three more sports to the lists in 2a, 2b and 3a. Tell your partner about your preferences, and say why. Find out if you have anything in common. Use the prompts below.

I play / used to play … I like / love / 'm passionate about … I have just taken up … I don't like / hate …

4a. Sporting events

Match the sporting events (1–6) to the sports (a–f).

1	Masters	a	football
2	Grand Prix	b	tennis
3	Olympics	c	athletics
4	World Cup	d	motor racing
5	Six Nations	e	rugby
6	Wimbledon	f	golf

> **Key word**
>
> **corporate hospitality** (noun): entertainment provided by companies for their customers in order to get more business
> **VIP** (noun): very important person: someone who receives special treatment because they are powerful or famous

4b. Speaking – corporate hospitality

You are going to take a VIP visitor to one of the sporting events in 4a. Pick an event and prepare to explain your choice to your boss.

See Module 3 Unit 4 for more on giving opinions and agreeing and disagreeing.

5. Game – questions of sport

Work in pairs. Take it in turns to choose one of the sports from the unit, then describe it to your partner without saying the name of the sport. Your partner can only ask questions that you can answer 'yes' or 'no' to. How many sports can you guess in five minutes?

'Is it an Olympic sport?'   'Is it a team sport?'   'Is it golf?'

6. Social planner

Now turn to the social planner on page 112 for more practice in this area.

Module 9 Unit 3
Talking about news and the media

In this unit, you will look at:

- news vocabulary
- news headlines and items
- adjectives to describe the media
- newspaper sections and types
- talking about the media
- talking about a news story

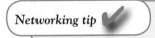 **Networking tip** ✔ | Often, something happens in the news that everyone is talking about. If you hear an interesting item on the news, it could be a good way to get people talking.

1. Vocabulary – collocations with 'news'

Look at the nine words and phrases related to the news. Put each one in the correct collocation box.

~~hear~~   listen to   breaking   catch up with   sports   latest   business   financial   international

Verbs	Adjectives	Nouns
hear the news	_____ news	_____ news
_____	_____	_____
_____	_____	_____
_____	_____	_____

2a. Vocabulary – in the headlines

Focus on these words and phrases connected with news stories. What subjects do they refer to? Put them into the correct categories: *Economy, Crime, Global warming* or *Employment*.

fraud   union   climate change   tax evasion   industrial dispute   credit crunch
kidnap   downturn   strike   temperatures   trial   hostage   prison

2b. Listening – headlines

🔘 **59** Listen to the news headlines. Write down the order in which you hear the six news items.

Finance ___ Crime ___ Colombian kidnap ___ Global warming ___ The weather ___ Strike ___

2c. Listening – news items

🔘 **60** Now listen to the news items in more detail and choose the correct options.

1 Schwarz <u>is / is not</u> in prison.
2 Global warming <u>does / does not</u> exist.
3 Strikes will <u>go ahead / not go ahead</u>.
4 The hostages are <u>dead / free</u>.
5 The economic downturn <u>should / should not</u> get worse.
6 Tomorrow's weather will be <u>good / bad</u>.

2d. News vocabulary

Check you know the meaning of the words in the box. Then use the correct form of these words to fill in the gaps in the extracts below.

rally   forecast   back down   accuse   rebel   evidence

Item 1: Schwartz is [1]_____ of cheating the German government out of 100,000 Euros.
Item 2: Scientists have announced new [2]_____ in the fight against climate change.
Item 3: The unions have finally [3]_____ in the long-running trade dispute in France.
Item 4: The five had been kidnapped by [4]_____ forces, and were feared dead.
Item 5: The markets are starting to [5]_____ and the downturn appears to be a thing of the past.
Item 6: And finally, the local weather [6]_____ for the next twenty-four hours.

60 When you have finished, listen again to the recording to check your answers.

3a. Vocabulary – media coverage

Tick the adjectives you would use to describe the media coverage in your country.

> unbiased   biased   critical   in-depth   superficial
> comprehensive   fair   accurate   balanced

Key word

the media (noun): radio, television, newspapers, the internet, and magazines, as a group

coverage (noun): the way in which something is reported on television, radio or in the newspapers

3b. Newspapers – sections

Match the newspaper 'sections' (1–8) to the descriptions (a–h).

1	domestic	a	industry and company news
2	business	b	news about famous people
3	editorial	c	opinion articles written by the head of the newspaper
4	celebrity gossip	d	the latest arts news
5	analysis	e	free time and hobbies
6	finance	f	local news
7	lifestyle	g	in-depth exploration of news stories
8	culture	h	update on the stock markets

3c. Newspapers – tabloids and broadsheets

There are two basic categories of newspapers: the 'tabloids' (less serious) and the 'broadsheets' (more serious). Look again at the newspaper sections 1–8 in 3b. Which sections are common in tabloids? Which are in broadsheets? Which are in both? Discuss your answers with a partner.

> **Cultural tip** ✔ In most countries newspapers take a certain political position. When talking about a story in a newspaper it can be very helpful to know or explain this position. For example: *This paper is left-wing / right-wing / in the centre* or *This paper usually supports / opposes the government.*

3d. Speaking – my media

Where do you get your news from? Tick the ones which apply to you. Compare your list with a partner and use the adjectives in exercise 3a to discuss the coverage of the different media.

TV ☐   Newspapers ☐   Magazines ☐   Radio ☐   Internet ☐   Blogs ☐

4. Writing & speaking – a news story

Find a news story. You can do this on the internet. Note down the following details:

What happened? Where did it happen? When did it happen? Who was involved? What was the coverage like?

Roleplay an appropriate networking situation, for example at a restaurant with a client or at a conference with a new associate. In three minutes, tell your partner about the story and the coverage, and get their opinion. Then change roles.

See also Module 3 Unit 4 on giving opinions, and Module 9 Unit 4 on dealing with controversial issues.

5. Social planner

Now fill in your social planner on page 112 with useful language associated with the media.

Module 9 Unit 4
Persuading and handling controversial topics

In this unit you will look at:

- types of arguments
- persuading phrases
- the language of controversy
- changing the topic

1a. Listening – persuading people

 61 We often want to 'persuade' someone to (make them believe) our own point of view. Listen to three dialogues. What are the people talking about? Circle the correct option for each one.

Dialogue 1: data projectors / interactive whiteboards   Dialogue 3: training sessions / meeting times
Dialogue 2: lifetime employment / moving abroad

1b. Ways of persuading – types of arguments

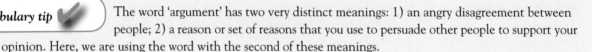
Vocabulary tip ✔ The word 'argument' has two very distinct meanings: 1) an angry disagreement between people; 2) a reason or set of reasons that you use to persuade other people to support your opinion. Here, we are using the word with the second of these meanings.

There are many ways of persuading people. Look at statements 1–3 below, which are three different ways of arguing the same point. Is each statement *emotional, rational* or *statistical*?

1 'If you don't support the project, lots of our own workers will lose their jobs. They won't be able to find work at their time of life. It could be that their families will go hungry.' _____

2 'If we invest now, all the market forecasts show that we will get a good profit.' _____

3 'It makes good economic sense to invest now. The markets are performing poorly so it seems clear that they will only get better.' _____

1c. Phrases – persuading

Put these words in the correct order to make useful 'persuading' phrases. The first one is an example.

1 you / don't / Why …? *Why don't you …?*
2 have / You / admit / to / that …

3 agree / Wouldn't / that / you …?
4 that / think / you / Don't …?

1d. Speaking – persuade the boss

Take it in turns to play the role of employee. Student A's roles are on page 81, student B's on page 84.

2a. Reading – guess the topic

Read the title and first line of the article below. What does it mean? What do you think the article will be about? Then read the article quickly and check if your prediction was correct.

2b. Reading – for key information

Read the article again and answer the questions: Who? When? Where? What happened? Why?

Too hot to handle?

Actress May Bee left last night's party in tears. She was talking to her manager, the host, Mel Gordon. Then, the conversation went terribly wrong. No one knows what they were talking about but first, both May and Mel became very emotional. Their gestures became more and more animated and lively. Their voices got louder and louder. Others said they couldn't understand why they didn't just change the subject.

Before continuing this unit, review the language of opinions in Module 3 Unit 4.

3a. Vocabulary – the language of controversy

Complete the gaps in the dictionary entries below with the correct adjective from the box.

| emotional | controversial | sensitive |

1 _____: causing disagreement or disapproval
2 _____: causing people to feel angry or upset quickly
3 _____: causing strong emotions, such as sadness and anger

Vocabulary tip ✔ Discussing or arguing? To 'discuss' has a positive meaning. People discuss problems, politics, economics and topics. To 'argue' has negative feelings connected with the word. People who argue can become angry. 'To have an argument' is often not a good thing.

3b. Listening – controversial topics

62 **Listen to the four discussions and put the topics in the correct order.**

Smoking in public places ____
ID cards ____
Digital downloads ____
Global warming ____

3c. Listening – changing the topic

62 **In each dialogue, someone comes in and suggests that the speakers change the subject. That person is acting as a 'peacemaker'. How did they change the topic? Listen again and tick any of the phrases below (a–l) that you hear, then try repeating them after the speakers.**

Commenting on a topic	Not commenting on a topic	Changing the topic
a It's quite a controversial topic.	e I'd prefer not to say.	i I think it's better not to talk about it.
b It's just one of those things.	f I'd rather not say.	j I think we should talk about something else.
c That's just the way it is.	g It's difficult to say.	k I think it's time to change conversation.
d It's a tricky one.	h I don't have an opinion one way or another.	l Let's change the topic.

4. Speaking – hot topics

Work in threes. Look at 'Hot topic 1' and the conversation map on page 84. Student A argues for the statement and student B argues against it: add further arguments to the ones given. Student C is the peacemaker: use the new language to keep the conversation from getting too 'hot'. Follow the map and talk for five minutes. Then change roles and repeat for the other two topics.

5. Social planner

Now turn to your social planner on page 112 for more practice with persuading.

Pairwork materials

Student A

Module 1 Unit 3 exercise 6b

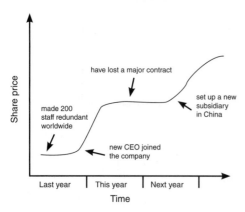

Module 1 Unit 4 exercise 2b

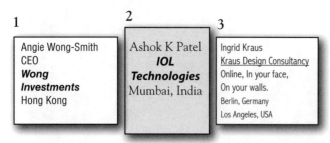

i   Work with a partner. Choose one of the business cards (1–3). Introduce yourself to your partner as the person on the card. Use the greeting dialogues as examples (look at listening script 7 on page 85 if necessary): try introducing yourself first in a formal way, and then less formally. Then choose another card and change roles.

ii Work with two partners. Choose two cards and introduce your partners to each other as the people on the cards. Change roles and choose two more cards.

iii If you have your own business card, introduce yourself to the other people in the class.

iv Introduce two other people in the class to each other, using their real details. Use the formal way first, then the informal way.

Module 3 Unit 2 exercise 6

Invite your partner to:

- a basketball match.
- dinner at your home on Thursday.
- see *Riverdance*.
- a local fish restaurant.
- visit the new shopping mall.

Use this information to accept or decline the invitations from your partner. Remember to be polite!

- You love Italian food.
- You find football boring.
- You have family visiting at the weekend.
- You are a big fan of Liza Minnelli.
- You aren't interested in antiques.

Module 4 Unit 1 exercise 5

You are in the hotel bar enjoying a drink. Student B enters the bar. You speak first.

1. Invite B to join you. (B speaks)
2. Offer to buy B a drink. (B speaks)
3. Order B's drink from the waiter (your teacher might play this role for you). (B speaks)
4. Describe your drink. (B speaks)
5. Agree, but say you are allergic to nuts. (B speaks)
6. Toast B. (B speaks)

Module 4 Unit 2 exercise 6

You are the host. Student B is a visiting client. You are in a restaurant in your country.

- invite B to choose something from the menu
- tell B what the local speciality is
- describe the local speciality to B
- if B can't eat this dish make another recommendation
- call the waiter (your teacher might play this role for you) and order lunch

Module 6 Unit 3 exercise 1d

Business card A (your card)

As a result of a major acquisition, the company is now called Central and Eastern European Aluminium SE. You have been promoted to Head of Marketing. Your email address is now ernst.schiller@ceealu.eu and your phone number 089 787 1963.

Business card B (student B's card)

> **Sally Fisher**
> Vice-president of sales: South America
> Alaska Oil Rigs Corp.
> 3320 14th Street
> New York, NY, USA
>
> Tel: 212 666 1002
> Email: sally_fisher@alaska-oil-rigs.com

Module 7 Unit 3 exercise 6

List of conversation topics:

the weather	a successful business deal	music
your country	the general economy	cars
your home town	current affairs	fashion
your job	your hobby or free time interests	food
your company	sport – playing or watching	drink
a recent business trip	cinema	the differences between countries
a recent holiday	books	your new house / flat

Module 7 Unit 4 exercise 7

1 **(5 minutes) Read the information about China below. Prepare to give this information to student B. If necessary, use a dictionary to check the meanings of any words you do not know. Be ready to clarify or rephrase any information or words student B does not understand, and use any of the phrases from the unit that you think are appropriate.**

China: Population: 1.6 billion – the largest in the world.
Main language: Mandarin, except: Hong Kong (Cantonese, English); Macao (Cantonese, Portuguese).
Industry: low-cost manufacturing, which is mostly private, and heavy industry, which is often state-owned.
Economy: fifth largest economy in the world.
Government: single-party system.

2 **(3 minutes) Explain your information to student B.**

3 **(3 minutes) Change roles and listen to student B's information. Use the new language from this unit to check and clarify what you hear and to make sure you have understood. Use an appropriate phrase to end the conversation.**

Module 8 Unit 2 exercise 5

1 You are feeling very confident.   2 You are feeling focused.   3 You are feeling defensive.

Module 9 Unit 4 exercise 1d

Read, prepare and act out roleplay 1. When you are finished, do the same for roleplay 2.

Roleplay 1: You want to persuade your boss to send you on a Caribbean sales trip. Your partner will play the role of your boss. First write down some arguments, using the prompts below. Use some of the expressions in 1c.
- good / sales
- new / opportunity
- increase / motivation
- come back / refreshed

Roleplay 2: Play the role of the boss for your partner's roleplay. You are not keen on giving him/her a pay rise. Write down some reasons why.

Student B

Module 1 Unit 3 exercise 6b

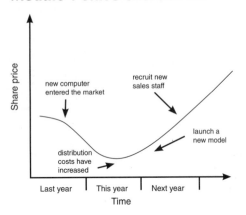

Module 1 Unit 4 exercise 2b

i   Work with a partner. Choose one of the business cards (4–6). Introduce yourself to your partner as the person on the card. Use the greeting dialogues as examples (look at listening script 7 on page 85 if necessary): try introducing yourself first in a formal way, and then less formally. Then choose another card and change roles.

ii Work with two partners. Choose two cards and introduce your partners to each other as the people on the cards. Change roles and choose two more cards.

iii If you have your own business card, introduce yourself to the other people in the class.

iv Introduce two other people in the class to each other, using their real details. Use the formal way first, then the informal way.

Module 3 Unit 2 exercise 6

Invite your partner to:

- a famous Italian restaurant.
- see Liza Minnelli in concert.
- visit the local antiques market.
- a football match.
- a barbeque at the weekend.

Use this information to accept or decline the invitations from your partner. Remember to be polite!

- You are allergic to seafood.
- You like basketball.
- You are free on Thursday evening.
- You hate folk dancing.
- You need to buy presents for your family.

Module 4 Unit 1 exercise 5

You enter a bar and see student A having a drink. A speaks first.

1. (A speaks) Accept the invitation.
2. (A speaks) Accept A's offer and choose a drink from the menu.
3. (A speaks) Ask A what they are drinking.
4. (A speaks) Suggest that you get some nibbles.
5. (A speaks) Order some olives from the waiter (your teacher might play this role for you).
6. (A speaks) Return the toast.

Module 4 Unit 2 exercise 6

You are the guest of student A, who is your supplier. You are visiting student A in his/her country. Student A will start the conversation.

- ask A what the local speciality is
- ask A to describe this dish
- give a reason why you can't eat the local speciality (be polite!)
- if A's second recommendation is good, thank A for the suggestion

Conference Programme

23rd International conference for personnel management, Oxford Business Centre, UK

9.00–10.00	**Keynote speech: Management today, success tomorrow** John Barrymore, Atlanta Business School	
10.15–11.00	1.1 **Managing difficult staff** George Tyson, USA George has 20 years' experience in personnel.	1.2 **Wearing different hats: an introduction to management styles** Carl Hansen Carl is an ex-manager at a well-known software firm. Now runs a management training company in Stockholm.
11.00	Coffee	
11.30–12.15	2.1 **Blended learning: the secrets of online training** Diana Phillips, Cork Diana has worked for a number of multinational companies and is a Blended Learning expert.	2.2 **Managing change: moving into the 21st century** Eunice May Eunice is a freelance consultant living and working in Calgary.
12.15–13.00	3.1 **Advanced interview skills** Mohammed Saif Mohammed runs an MBA course in Cairo.	Lunch
13.00–13.45	Lunch	3.2 **Motivation, motivation, motivation** Jenny Holmes, Edinburgh Updating last year's successful session.
14.00–15.00	4.1 **Developing staff portfolios using technology** Julio Aragon, Sao Paolo Julio is an expert in new technology.	4.2 **Leadership skills** Claire Peacock Based in York, Claire is a leading figure in management training.
15.00	Tea and biscuits	
15.30–16.15	5.1 **Making personnel personal: appraising people** Tim Wright, Oxford Business Centre Tim is a management trainer.	5.2 **An introduction to team-building** Martha Prince, Paris Business Centre A practical seminar useful for anyone working in a team.
16.30–17.15	6.1 **Running an in-service training programme** Jeremy Small, Luxemburg This session builds on the ideas presented in Jeremy's new book.	6.2 **Managing conflict in the workplace** Juan Alberto Espinosa Juan works in Madrid as a business skills trainer.
17.30–18.00	Raffle / closing ceremony	

Conference planner

9.00 –10.00	Keynote: Management today, success tomorrow (Barrymore)
10.15–11.00	Session one:
11.00	Coffee
11.30–12.15	Session two:
12.15–13.00	Lunch or 3.1:
13.00–13.45	Lunch or 3.2:
14.00–15.00	Session four:
15.00	Tea and biscuits
15.30–16.15	Session five:
16.30–17.15	Session six:

Business card A (student A's card)

> **Ernst Schiller**
> Assistant Manager – Marketing
>
> Central European Aluminium SE
> Nord Strasse 56
> Munich
> Germany
>
> Tel: 089 777 7059
> Email: e.schiller1@cealu.de

Business card B (your card)

The company has moved to 2460 11th Street. You are now responsible for Africa and South-East Asia. You recently got married to Lance Mankolinowitz and took his surname.

Module 7 Unit 4 exercise 7

1 (5 minutes) Read the information about Brazil below. Prepare to give this information to student A. If necessary, use a dictionary to check the meanings of any words you do not know. Be ready to clarify or rephrase any information or words student A does not understand, and use any of the phrases from the unit that you think are appropriate.

Brazil: Population: 190 million – fifth largest in the world.
Main language: Portuguese – most other South American countries speak Spanish.
Industry: agriculture, mining, manufacturing, and is an important producer of oil.
Economy: tenth largest in the world, the largest in South America.
Government: democratic government with a president – the current constitution dates from 1988.

2 (3 minutes) Listen to student A's information. Use the new language from this unit to check and clarify what you hear and to make sure you have understood. Use an appropriate phrase to end the conversation.

3 (3 minutes) Change roles and explain your information to student A.

Module 8 Unit 2 exercise 5

1 You are feeling very nervous.   2 You are feeling relaxed.   3 You are feeling engaged.

Module 9 Unit 4 exercise 1d

Read, prepare and act out roleplay 1. When you are finished, do the same for roleplay 2.

Roleplay 1: Play the role of the boss for your partner's roleplay. You are not keen on sending him/her on a Caribbean sales trip. Write down some reasons why.

Roleplay 2: You want to persuade your boss to give you a pay rise. Your partner will be your boss. First write down some arguments, using the prompts below. Use some of the expressions in 1c.
- deserve it
- work unpaid overtime
- motivating
- value of salary lower because of credit crunch

Module 9 Unit 4 exercise 4

Hot topic 1: Men's and women's salaries should be equal	Hot topic 2: Big bonuses should not be allowed	Hot topic 3: There should be unrestricted internet access at work
Student A: Equal jobs should mean equal salaries. Student B: When a woman has a family, she takes time out of her job. Who pays? The company. Student C: Peacemaker.	Student A: It is ridiculous that banks make so much money. Student B: In a capitalist system it is motivating to be rewarded financially for hard work. Student C: Peacemaker.	Student A: It is helpful for work and keeps employees motivated. Student B: Workers would waste time surfing the internet when they should be working. Student C: Peacemaker.

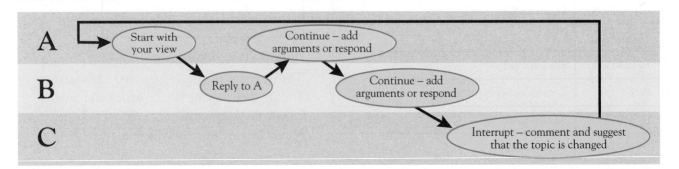

Listening scripts

Module 1

Unit 1

 1

Marc: Where are you are from, Ingrid?
Ingrid: Originally? Hamburg, Germany.
Marc: Really? I have to say, your accent doesn't sound very German.
Ingrid: Well, I did go to high school in the United States for two years.
Marc: I see. Where in the US was that?
Ingrid: In New Jersey. It was a good experience. I learnt a lot.
Marc: And did you go to university in the US?
Ingrid: No, I studied industrial design back in Germany, in Berlin.
Marc: A-ha. So, when did you decide to change to graphic design?
Ingrid: I started doing design work for people in Berlin while I was at university. I designed some websites for some local companies and a few books.
Marc: And when did you become a freelance consultant?
Ingrid: It was in 2006 while I was doing my master's degree. I was developing a client base in Germany and then I got some work from a friend in the US.
Marc: Mm-hm. Did you stay at university?
Ingrid: Of course. In the US they are more interested in what you can do but in Europe, people prefer to see your qualifications before they ask about your experience.
Marc: That's true. When did you graduate?
Ingrid: In 2007.
Marc: And which do you prefer, Europe or the US?
Ingrid: Oh, I can't really say. They've both got their pros and cons.

 2

I am from Germany. I'm from Germany.
I do not live in Hamburg anymore. I don't live in Hamburg anymore.
We are setting up an office in New York. We're setting up an office in New York.
She has just got a promotion. She's just got a promotion.

Unit 2

 3

(see unit for the sentences)

 4

Ashok: How was your flight, Brad?
Brad: It was good. I'm still a little confused by the time difference though.
Ashok: That's always a difficulty with going from continent to continent. Do you travel

much?
Brad: Not so much, although this is my second time in India.
Ashok: Really? I didn't know. Was that for business or were you on holiday?
Brad: It was a vacation. It was great – we got to see so many famous places. You know, the Taj Mahal, a bunch of places in Delhi and then we took the train to Varanasi.
Ashok: Did you visit Mumbai?
Brad: No, I really wanted to, but I ran out of time. How about you? Have you been to the US?
Ashok: Yes. I spent two years in Boston.
Brad: Two years! How come?
Ashok: I was studying for an MBA. I have never been to Los Angeles though. Is it very different from Boston?
Brad: Oh yes. It's almost hard to believe that they're in the same country. People tell me Boston's more like Europe.
Ashok: Have you been to Europe?
Brad: No, not yet. I'm going there after I leave India. I'm spending a couple of days in London then I'm going to the movie festival in Berlin. How about you?
Ashok: I go the UK quite often. In fact, my wife is from Edinburgh.
Brad: She's Scottish?
Ashok: By birth, yes. But her father is my mother's cousin.
Brad: I see, I think.
Ashok: It's quite common in Indian culture to marry a cousin. We often have very big and complicated families.
Brad: Have you got any kids?
Ashok: No, not yet. We only got married about nine months ago. How about you? Are you married?
Brad: No. I'm currently free and single. I guess I'm married to my work at the moment.

Unit 3

 5

Ashok: I set up my first company with another student on my MBA course.
Brad: What exactly do you do?
Ashok: Computer programming for commercial websites and other online applications. All of our clients are in the US and Canada.
Brad: So how many folks do you employ?
Ashok: At the moment, we have a couple of salespeople in the US, plus my partner. Then there's me and sixteen programmers here in Mumbai.
Brad: Sixty programmers! That's a big operation.
Ashok: No not six zero, one six. Sixteen.
Brad: Sixteen! I'm sorry, I misheard. Is it OK to ask how much you're making?
Ashok: Last year we turned over about two million dollars, which gave us a profit of a

little over two hundred thousand dollars.
Brad: That's not bad for a two-year-old company. How many clients do you have?
Ashok: About fifty in total.
Brad: That's five zero, right?
Ashok: Yes, that's right.

 6

Thirteen / Thirty.
Fourteen / Forty.
Fifteen / Fifty.
Sixteen / Sixty.
Seventeen / Seventy.
Eighteen / Eighty.
Nineteen / Ninety.

Unit 4

 7

a
Angie: How do you do? I'm Angie Wong-Smith from Wong Investments.
Ingrid: Pleased to meet you, Mrs Wong-Smith. I'm Ingrid Kraus, I'm a designer.
Angie: How are you, Ms Kraus?
Ingrid: Very well, thank you. And you?
Angie: I'm fine. Thank you for asking.
b
Ashok: Good morning Brad.
Brad: Morning Ashok. How you doing?
Ashok: I'm fine. What about you?
Brad: I'm good.
c
Angie: Hello Claire!
Claire: Hello Angie. It's lovely to see you. How long has it been?
Angie: It must be nearly two years. It was at that conference in Nice, wasn't it?
Claire: Yes, you're right. Doesn't time fly. How are you?
Angie: I'm very well indeed. And you?
Claire: I'm much better now, thanks.
Angie: That's good to hear.

8

1
Brad: OK Ashok, I'll catch you tomorrow.
Ashok: Good night Brad. See you in the morning.
Brad: Ciao.
2
Claire: Well, Angie, it was lovely to see you again.
Angie: You too Claire. It was wonderful to catch up.
Claire: I'll see you again before you fly back to Hong Kong.
Angie: Of course. Bye for now.
Claire: Take care. Bye-bye.
3
Ingrid: It was nice meeting you, Mrs Wong-Smith.
Angie: It was nice meeting you too, Ms Kraus. Thank you again for coming.
Ingrid: Goodbye.
Angie: Goodbye. Have a safe journey.

Module 2

Unit 1

 9

1 I often go on package holidays to Dubai and South Africa. And flying over Africa is a magical experience – but only if you have a window seat on the plane!

2 Hmmm – Last year, I went to a conference in Mexico, so I took the opportunity to travel around and see the country at the same time. I made some great contacts and saw some amazing things. Mind you, the traffic jams were shocking!

3 When I left school, my friend and I went on a camping trip to Canada. It was lovely – I'll never forget it. Nowadays I hate flying – so my holidays tend to be a little closer to home.

4 Can you believe it, I've never been to France! But I'm thinking of popping over there on a budget airline the next time I'm in London.

Unit 2

 10

Marc: You know Edinburgh, don't you Ashok? What do you advise me to do when I'm there?

Ashok: Yes, my wife grew up there. Here's a map of the city centre. Obviously, you must visit Princes Street. It's just north of the gardens and quite long. You should see the famous statue, here – Scott's Monument – near the end of Princes Street. The castle's also very impressive. It's here, overlooking Princes Street Gardens, not far from your hotel.

Marc: The castle is on a hill, isn't it?

Ashok: Yes it is, but you can easily walk it. And whatever you do, don't miss the Royal Mile. It's this long street that heads east from the Castle. Do you like art?

Marc: Of course. I am French!

Ashok: There are so many museums and galleries in Edinburgh … actually, I'd recommend visiting the Royal Museum of Scotland. It's here, just south of Cowgate. I think you'd enjoy it. And down here at the end of Queen's Drive and the Royal Mile is Holyrood Palace. It's beautiful.

Marc: OK. Thanks very much, Ashok. That sounds great.

Ashok: I'm sure you'll have a lovely time. Don't forget to take your camera!

 11

1 The best time to visit is in the spring. The weather is warm and you can see the famous cherry blossoms … The temples are top of my list of sightseeing highlights. You can get to some of them by bullet train, the Shinkansen. They reach speeds of up to 300 kilometres per hour … Did you change any money at the airport? They use the yen. I'll be able to tell you the latest exchange rate.

2 It's such a huge country. Most tourists come to see the Great Wall of course. And did you know that Shanghai is actually the largest city? … Anyway, it's wonderful that you are here for the spectacular New Year celebrations – we hold many festivals all over the country.

3 What's typical? I think that Bavaria in the south is very different from where I live, in Hamburg. Many countries have a north-south divide. If you do get to Munich, try the schweinshaxe. It's a classic Bavarian dish. I must say, it's not for me though – I'm a vegetarian.

4 When we say the UK, we mean Great Britain – which is England, Scotland and Wales – plus Northern Ireland… Of course everyone asks what they should take back home with them. I'm from near London so I always say the same thing: marmalade and tea. If you come from north of the border, though, I guess the answer might be a bottle of malt whisky!

Unit 3

 12

Brad: I think I'll skip the main course, Marc. Just a light, green salad for me.

Marc: I have to say I'm impressed by the way you always choose a healthy option, Brad. How do you do it?

Brad: It's quite easy really, I guess. I just avoid those things that are obviously bad for you, like fried foods, burgers and fatty meats. I'm just sensible. When it comes to dairy products, like cream and cheese, I always go for the low-fat versions. We have low-fat everything in the States.

Marc: I admire your discipline. I know I could never cut out cheese. But I imagine you still eat meat?

Brad: Well, yes, but I try to avoid red meat and rich sauces.

Marc: But French sauces are wonderful, Brad! You only live once.

Brad: Sure. But five portions of fruit and vegetables a day are good for you. And drinking plenty of water of course.

Marc: OK then, let's order some more water. Now, where's the wine list?

Unit 4

 13

Welcome to John Smiths plc. It's a great company to work for. First of all, John, that's John Peacock, our Chief Executive Officer, sends his apologies as he can't be here to welcome you today. … So let's start with finance. Maria Wong, the finance director, is in charge of the department. Then we have Rebecca Sharpe and her team of accountants. Rebecca's the chief accountant and keeps everyone in check. Then it gets a bit complicated because Shaun Barrett, the payroll clerk, actually answers to both Maria and Rebecca. …The sales team all deal with different tasks, but ultimately they answer to Lynette Strong, the sales director. Carl Wiseman, the sales executive, works for Lynette and alongside Jane Robson, our marketing manager. Jane's responsible for advertising and she's absolutely brilliant – I really don't know what we'd do without her. … Some other important people in the company are Michael Stanley, our Research and Development manager, who helps us stay at the top with his innovative work, and David Rice, who is head of IT. … But first let's go to the personnel department to meet Daniel Logan. He's the personnel manager and he needs to speak to you about filling in a joining form. Oh, how silly, I forgot to introduce myself. I'm Martha Ivers, company secretary. I'm not really involved in human resources, but around here you get used to doing quite a few different jobs. Once again, welcome to John Smiths plc.

Module 3

Unit 1

 14

(see unit for the sentences)

 15

Angie: You travel a lot for work, don't you Marc?

Marc: Yes, but I really don't like it.

Angie: Really, why's that?

Marc: Well, it's not the same as being a tourist. I have no time to go sightseeing. I fly in, I go to the hotel, I have meetings all day. The only things that are different from France are the weather and the awful food.

Angie: I am surprised to hear that. So how do you spend your holidays?

Marc: I prefer to stay at home with my family. I like to go riding with my wife and my daughters and I like to have dinner at my friend's restaurant.

Angie: Do you never go away?

Marc: Sometimes we go skiing for a week.

Angie: Do you like skiing?

Marc: I quite like it but I prefer riding. How about you? You must like to travel. You're always flying around the world. Where is your favourite place?

Angie: It's difficult to say really. It's probably Shanghai, although it's a bit of a love / hate relationship at the moment. I really like the dynamism and the optimism of the people and the way the city is always changing. Plus it's not far from Hong Kong of course. On the other hand, I hate the noise and the pollution.

Marc: Don't you also have an apartment in New York?

Angie: Yes, a small one near Central Park.

Marc: So which city do you prefer?

Angie: I will always love New York but Shanghai is where everything's happening right now. In fact, I predict it will soon overtake New York as the centre of global business.

Unit 2

 16

Claire: Would you like to come for dinner one evening? See my new place?

Ingrid: I'd like that very much. When did you have in mind?

Claire: I was thinking of Thursday evening. Does that suit you?

Ingrid: Thursday is fine for me.

Claire: Good. Let's say seven thirty for eight, then.

Ingrid: Sorry? I don't follow.

Claire: Well, if you aim to arrive at around half past seven, we'll have some drinks and then dinner will be at eight.

Ingrid: Oh, I see. How did you say it again? Seven thirty for eight?

Claire: Yes, that's right.

Ingrid: Should I bring anything? I've never been to a dinner party in the UK.

Claire: Well, you don't have to but it's traditional to bring a bottle of wine or some chocolates.

Ingrid: That's the same in Germany.

Claire: Oh, and I've also invited my friend Angie Wong-Smith. She's the financier from Hong Kong I told you about. She's really keen to meet you.

Ingrid: Oh, that's really exciting. I'm looking forward to meeting her too.

Claire: Do you know how to find us?

Ingrid: I have your address. I can get a taxi from the station.

Claire: Great. See you on Thursday then.

Unit 3

 17

Brad: Ingrid, tell me about Berlin.

Ingrid: What do you want to know?

Brad: Well, I'm going to the film festival in February, but I haven't booked a hotel yet. Can you recommend a reasonably priced one?

Ingrid: Well, the festival takes place around Potsdamer Platz. I suggest you book a room at the Novotel. It's really close to the centre of the city and if you book early, you might get a discount.

Brad: That sounds good, thanks. Now, I've promised to take this Swiss financier out one night. Can you suggest a good place for dinner? Somewhere with excellent food but not too swanky.

Ingrid: That's easy. I can recommend a very exclusive restaurant in the east of the city. Here's the phone number. My friend runs it so mention my name when you make the booking.

Brad: That's fabulous, Ingrid. Oh, and I've also scheduled some time to be a tourist. What do you think I should do?

Ingrid: If this is your first trip, you should take a bus tour. You buy a ticket and you can get on and off when you want. You can even hear the descriptions in English. That way you can see the most famous places like the Reichstag Building and the Brandenburg Gate. From the outside at least.

Brad: That's a really good idea. Thanks very much. Oh yes! And I have to get something for my mom and dad. What's a typical souvenir from Berlin?

Ingrid: If I were you, I would get them something from the Ampelmann Shop in Potsdamer Platz. The little traffic light man is a modern symbol of the city.

Unit 4

 18

Angie: Marc, what do you think about the European Union? Is it a good thing?

Marc: Well, the European Union has created peace in Europe for over fifty years.

Angie: I can see that but my question was more about business and economics.

Marc: Well, of course, there are many benefits to having an economic union but also several drawbacks.

Angie: For example?

Marc: I think it is now too big. It seems to me that it's getting bigger every year. I'm convinced that the original French vision of a small group of countries with similar cultures and the same currency, taxes and social and economic system was far better than what we have today.

Angie: So why didn't it happen?

Marc: Some people ignored the rules.

Angie: But shouldn't the EU try to find a balance between the needs of its members?

Marc: Maybe, but from my point of view the more centralized it is the better.

Angie: What about the Euro? What do you think about that?

Marc: I completely agree with the introduction of the Euro but it would really be better if it was used by everyone.

Angie: But in general, how do you feel about the future of the EU?

Marc: I think we will have more unity in the future and I am sure the EU will be in an important position to do good business with other parts of the world.

Angie: Thanks Marc. It's a complicated issue so I find it useful to hear what Europeans think about it.

 19

(see unit for the sentences)

Module 4

Unit 1

 20

Ingrid: What about this place? Quiet and not too crowded.

Brad: I thought we could find a place where we can listen to some music.

Ingrid: And I thought we were going to have a chat about Marc's proposal. We can't do that if there's music blasting out.

Brad: I guess you're right. This place doesn't seem to have very much atmosphere though.

Ingrid: It's a traditional English pub. Come on, it'll be interesting.

Brad: OK then. Do you want to sit at the bar or shall we find a table?

Ingrid: A table would be better but we have to go to the bar first to order a drink. They don't have waiters in pubs.

Brad: They don't?! We do in the US.

Ingrid: And in Germany, but not in the UK. What would you like?

Brad: I don't know. I don't recognize anything.

Ingrid: Well, this is a French beer, this one is Irish and these two here are typically British.

Brad: You seem to be an expert!

Ingrid: I'm not. I hate beer. I had a boyfriend in London for a short time. We spent a lot of time in pubs.

Brad: Oh, I see. Well, I think I'll try a British beer. A pint of this one please. What about you?

Ingrid: I'm going to have a cup of coffee.

Brad: Oh Ingrid! We're in a pub. You can't have coffee.

Ingrid: I really don't drink Brad. Hey, let's get some nibbles.

Brad: Some what?

Ingrid: Nibbles. They're snacks like crisps or nuts. Oh look! Pork scratchings.

Brad: What are they?!

Ingrid: I don't know. Let's try some.

 21

(see unit for the sentences)

Unit 2

 22

Ashok: What do you fancy, Brad? Have you tried Indian before?

Brad: I went to an Indian in Boston but the menu looked different to this one.

Ashok: That's often the case. My uncle has a restaurant in Los Angeles and had to adapt to local tastes and ingredients.

Brad: So, what should I order?

Ashok: That depends. Are you a vegetarian?

Brad: I'm what they call a 'Californian vegetarian', which basically means I don't eat red meat.
Ashok: Well you won't find any beef on the menu here, I promise.
Brad: Really? Oh, because it's against your religion, right?
Ashok: That's right. Do you like spicy food?
Brad: We eat a lot of Mexican food in California so I like it pretty hot.
Ashok: That's good.
Brad: Is there a local speciality?
Ashok: Oh yes, lots. I suggest we order several dishes so that you can sample a few different things.
Brad: Sounds excellent.

Unit 3

 23

Claire: Don't forget to put your name badge on.
Ashok: Oh yes, thank you. Have you studied the conference programme? What are you going to go to?
Claire: Well, John Barrymore from Atlanta is giving the keynote speech on the future of personnel management.
Ashok: You've seen him before haven't you? Is he any good?
Claire: Yes. He's a very dynamic speaker. He's got lots of fascinating ideas.
Ashok: The talk on blended learning looks interesting. I should go to that but it's on at the same time as Eunice May's talk about managing change.
Claire: Hmm. Personally, I'd go to Eunice's talk. She always has something new to say.
Ashok: Hmm, it's a tricky one … but on balance I think the blended learning talk is probably more relevant to my job. What about the afternoon?
Claire: I'm going to Jeremy Small's workshop on in-service training. That's important for my job.
Ashok: Me too. What's he like?
Claire: I don't really know, but his presentation sounds promising.
Ashok: Oh look, it's nearly nine o'clock.
Claire: Oh yes, so it is. Where's John Barrymore giving his talk?
Ashok: In the main auditorium, I think. We'd better hurry.

Unit 4

 24

Secretary: Mr Ruby is here.
Ashok: Ah Brad, come through. It's good to see you again, my friend.
Brad: You too, Ashok. How are you doing?
Ashok: Very well, thanks. And yourself?
Brad: A little jet-lagged, but I'm good.
Ashok: You can put your bag over there. Come and sit down.
Brad: Thank you.

Ashok: Can I get you something to drink: tea, coffee, water?
Brad: Can I have a glass of water, please?
Ashok: Gita, could you bring us some tea and a glass of water for Mr Ruby? So Brad, did you find our new offices OK?
Brad: Yes, no problem. They're a bit different from your old building.
Ashok: Yes, now we have more clients we needed something more modern. Ah, here's the tea and your glass of water. Oh, by the way, Marc telephoned a few minutes ago to say he's on his way. So, how was your journey?

Claire: Hello Ingrid, you're right on time. Come in.
Ingrid: Good evening Claire, thank you.
Claire: Here, let me take your coat. How are you?
Ingrid: Very well, thanks. This is for you.
Claire: Châteauneuf-du-Pape. Oh, thank you Ingrid. That's my favourite. Come into the sitting room.
Ingrid: What a beautiful room. Oh, and that painting is fabulous.
Claire: Yes, isn't it wonderful. Would you like a drink? Angie's on her way, she'll be here soon.
Ingrid: Yes please.
Claire: What about white wine? I've got a nice bottle of English in the fridge.
Ingrid: Oh yes, just a little then. Thanks.
Claire: Make yourself comfortable, I'll just be a moment.

Module 5

Unit 1

 25

Marc: So, Angie. What's your favourite city? Where would you like to live?
Angie: Oh that's difficult. Barcelona, maybe. No, wait – it's got to be New York. It's much more exciting than anywhere else I can think of.
Marc: Oh, I don't agree. Did you know in London you can eat out at a restaurant from every country in the world? And it's the same in Paris.
Angie: Yes, but London's so much busier. It's more crowded and dirtier than most capital cities – and it's MUCH more expensive than most other places!
Marc: Expensive? What about Tokyo?!
Angie: Hmm, good point. So, what about you? What's your favourite city?
Marc: Angie! Paris – of course. It's more romantic than anywhere else I know.

Unit 3

26

(see unit for the words)

1
Speaker A: So that's the end of the conference call. We'll meet again next Tuesday, the 23rd. Is that OK?
Speaker B: I'm sorry. Could you say that again a bit more slowly?
2
A: I loved the part of the presentation about tort. How about you?
B: Sorry – what does 'tort' mean?
A: Oh – er, it's a legal word. It means when you do something wrong, and it causes an injury.
B: Oh, yes, I think I understand.
3
A: I wouldn't touch it with a bargepole!
B: Pardon? What did you say?
A: I mean – I just wouldn't go anywhere near it. Sorry, us Brits use a lot of, er …
B: Idioms?
A: Yeah – that's the one. I guess you have them in your own language, right?
4
A: Haw wah there, my friend.
B: I'm sorry. What did you say?
A: Och, don't mind me lad. I do have a bit of a Scottish accent but not much.
5
A: Let's have a gander.
B: I'm sorry. I don't understand.
A: I mean, let me have a look. Sorry, we do use rather a lot of, er, slang.
B: Slang?
A: You know – colloquial language – like real people use.
6
A: I wouldn't've done that.
B: Sorry – what did you say?
A: I said, I would not have done that.
B: Ah, yes. Would not, wouldn't.

28

1
Paul: OK, so we hope to ship the goods to you on the first of next month. I assume that's OK, John?
John: OK.
Paul: Great. The terms of delivery are pretty well as we discussed. You're giving us a longer delivery time, and we're going to give you a thirty per cent discount. I hope that's fine with you guys. What do you think, John?
John: Oh, yes, OK. Er, I think it's OK.
Paul: Great. Now, who's up for dinner?
2
Paul: OK, so we hope to ship the goods to you on the first of next month. I assume that's OK, Sandra?
Sandra: So, let me just check that … You're sending us the goods on the first day of next

month, March?
Paul: Yes, that's right. I hope that's OK?
Sandra: Yes, that's fine.
Paul: Great. The terms of delivery are pretty well as we discussed. You're giving us a longer delivery time, and we're going to give you a thirty per cent discount. I hope that's fine with you guys. What do you think, Sandra?
Sandra: I'm sorry, I didn't quite catch that. Could you go over that again?
Paul: Sure. I said you're giving us a longer delivery time, and we're going to give you a thirty per cent discount.
Sandra: Ahh, yes. Let me jot that down. A ... longer ... delivery ... time. Yes, that's fine. About the discount – I think we said thirteen per cent, didn't we?
Paul: Of course we did – I'm sorry. Thirteen per cent it is.
Sandra: Perfect. Please could you email over the terms tomorrow and I'll draw up the documentation.
Paul: Great, will do. Now, who's up for dinner?

 29

1
A: It was such an awful day. My car broke down on the way to work. Then at work, I tried to turn on the computer and it was completely on the blink. After that, my boss told me I'll have to look for another job. Can you believe it?
B: Believe what? Sorry, I was just trying to get this email off. What was that?
2
A: It was such an awful day.
B: Oh no. Why?
A: My car broke down on the way to work.
B: Oh dear. That's awful.
A: Then at work, I tried to turn on the computer and it was completely on the blink.
B: Sorry, on the blink?
A: I mean it wouldn't work.
B: Oh, I see. I think the network's down.
A: After that, my boss told me I'll have to look for another job. Can you believe it?
B: Oh dear. I'm so sorry. Is there anything I can do?
3
A: It was such an awful day. My car broke down on the way to work.
B: (Tut.)
A: Then at work, I tried to turn on the computer and it was completely on the blink.
B: Oh no.
A: After that, my boss told me I'll have to look for another job. Can you believe it?
B: Oh.

Unit 2

 30

Marc: Did you read about that report on the world economy?
Angie: Well, yes. It was all over the newspapers last week.
Ashok: And the Web.
Claire: Do you mean the one about the effects of the credit crunch? What exactly did it say? I only skimmed the coverage.
Marc: It said that the credit crunch was good for the economy, but in my opinion it didn't consider the human cost.
Angie: Well, I think it did have some positive results. The markets were overvalued and banking practices needed to change. Looking back, it was inevitable.
Marc: I agree that the situation could not continue but why did we have to wait until everything crashed before governments responded?
Claire: It was a horrible period.
Marc: You both work in banking. Why did no one see it coming?
Angie: You can't really blame Claire and me for what happened, Marc. Even up to the end of 2007 things still seemed good. Everything had been going up for years: the stock exchange, property prices, bonuses. We all thought the good times would go on forever.
Claire: Even when there seemed to be warnings, people didn't really take any notice.
Marc: So when **did** the bankers start to take notice? At the end of 2008, banks were falling all over the place and governments started putting together rescue packages using billions of our money.
Angie: Well, the IMF gave a warning in April, I think it was.
Claire: And in the UK property prices were falling, which is always a sign of economic problems.
Angie: I think the wake-up call was when Lehman Brothers Bank went bankrupt in September and after that it was one bank after another.
Ashok: Was that when the recession started?
Angie: Yes, it was officially announced in the US at the end of the year.
Marc: The bottom fell out of our business. All over the world, clients cancelled projects with my company; they couldn't get money from the banks. It didn't matter what stage our projects were at, everything stopped. We had to lay off hundreds of workers all over the world.
Claire: I experienced that too, Marc. The bosses of the bank panicked and we were told to cut the workforce by half over one weekend. As head of human resources I had to tell so many people they had to leave the company.

Angie: I was desperate to invest in companies and people but it was just impossible to make loans. Everybody in banking was terrified of lending money. They had so many bad debts that they didn't trust anyone.
Claire: But then in 2009 all those international rescue packages were agreed.
Marc: More public money down the drain.
Angie: Be fair, Marc. We all need banks. There was no choice. They had to be rescued. And things are getting better now, aren't they?
Marc: I suppose so. In fact our business has changed. We now have lots of infrastructure projects instead of private ones. It's an interesting time.
Angie: And banks are lending again. What do you think Claire?
Claire: Hmm, I'm definitely optimistic – at least we're recruiting now. Ashok, you've been very quiet. What was your experience of the credit crunch?
Ashok: Oh, it's a bit embarrassing. We did really well. Because companies rushed to cut their costs, even more American and European companies started sourcing their IT services from India. My company doubled in size during the first half of 2009.

Unit 3

 31

Claire: Let me give you my business card, Ashok. Just a second.
Ashok: Thank you Claire. Here's mine.
Claire: Thank you very much. Could you put it on the table for the moment? Thanks. Here you are. Oh, damn!
Ashok: Is there a problem?
Claire: Yes, I'm sorry – this is one of my old cards. We've just been taken over by BGB Bank so the information on this card is mostly out of date. My new cards must be in my hotel room.
Ashok: That's OK, you can write your new contact details on the back of your old one. There's space here.
Claire: Do you mind doing it? My hands are full at the moment.
Ashok: No problem. Go ahead.
Claire: My new email address is Claire, that's Claire with an 'i', dot Thanet at BGB Bank, all one word, dot com.
Ashok: Sorry, could you say that again a little slower?
Claire: Certainly. Claire, as it's written there: C-L-A-I-R-E. Dot. Thanet: T-H-A-N-E-T. At BGB Bank – and that's written as a single word – dot com.
Ashok: OK, so that's Claire dot Thanet at BGB Bank dot com.
Claire: That's right. And my phone number is now 020 472 00349.
Ashok: 020 472 0349.
Claire: No. Two 'o's.

Ashok: Sorry?
Claire: It ends 00349. With two 'o's.
Ashok: Oh, I see. So that's 020 472 00349.
Is that right?
Claire: Yes, that's right. That's the direct line to my office. My work mobile is the same but let me give you my personal mobile just in case. It's 0734 204 9090.
Ashok: Just a second. 0734 204 9090.
Claire: That's right.

 32

Marc: Is that a mobile phone, Brad?
Brad: Yes, it's an iPhone. Everybody in our company has one.
Angie: Can I have a look?
Brad: Sure. Here you are.
Angie: Oh, it's very light.
Brad: Yeah. Less than 5 ounces.
Marc: I don't know how much that is.
Brad: I dunno, maybe 150 grams.
Marc: I see.
Brad: So, it's got this three-and-a-half-inch touch-sensitive screen that controls everything.
Angie: Like this? Oh, that's really easy.
Brad: Yeah, that's it. The network's 3G of course so I can get fast internet access almost anywhere. It can play 12 different digital movie formats. And it's got 30 gigabytes of memory so I can store several hours of video.
Marc: That's very impressive.
Brad: I use it to manage all my contacts and email. It can handle 30 different file formats so I can read any attachment.
Angie: Useful when you're travelling.
Brad: It sure is. And it's got a 3-megapixel camera. So I can take your photo like this. Smile.
Angie: And you can make phone calls?
Brad: Sure. You do this and, oh rats!
Marc: What's the matter?
Brad: I got no signal.

 33

Ingrid: So, how do I get to the restaurant?
Claire: It's easy. Turn right out of the office building and follow the street to the end then turn left. You then go straight before taking the first road on the right.
Angie: Is it the first road on the right? What about Angel Street? That's the first turning on the right.
Claire: Yes, you're right. So, don't take the first road on the right, take the second.
Ingrid: Is that Angel Street?
Angie: No, it's Westminster Street. Angel Street takes you to the car park.
Claire: You turn right into Westminster Street and go about a hundred metres.
Angie: More like a hundred and fifty.
Claire: Well, you go straight until you see the post office on your right. Sort of opposite that is a narrow little road. You need to go up there.

Angie: Are you sure that's the quickest way? Surely it's better to continue down Westminster Street and turn left up Oxford Road. Those little back streets are so confusing.
Claire: Well you can go the Oxford Road way but it's much longer, I think. Are you with me so far, Ingrid?
Ingrid: I think so. I …
Claire: So you go up this narrow road.
Ingrid: Oxford Road?
Claire: No, Oxford Road is the main road. I forget the name of this one. You walk about fifty metres and there is a little street on your right. You can't miss it, there's a tiny craft shop on the corner that sells things from India. Go a few metres down that little street, but don't go as far as the square. The restaurant is on your left, just next to the shoe shop.
Angie: And if you walk straight through the square, you get to Oxford Road.
Claire: Did you follow that?
Ingrid: I think I've got it. Let me see whether I can repeat it.

 34

Ingrid: So, I go out of this office building, turn right and walk to the end of the street and turn left. I take the second turning on the right, which is called Westminster Street. There is a post office on the right side of Westminster Street and opposite that is a narrow road. I should follow that road until I find a little craft shop on the corner of a little street. I go down the little street, which takes me to a square. The restaurant is on the left, just before the square, next to the shoe shop. Is that right?
Claire: That's perfect. Are you sure you've never been there before?

Unit 4

 35

1
A: Are you working?
B: Oh, erm, I'm not walking.
A: No, I mean working.
2
A: I'd like to buy a ramp.
B: I'm sorry – this is a lamp shop.
3
A: I love chass.
B: Sorry, do you mean 'chess'?
4
A: The toilets are on floor B.
B: Pardon? Did you say P?

 36

(see unit for the words)

 37

(see unit for the sentences)

 38

1   What will happen to them?

2   I've not met her.
3   I'm so tired.

 39

(see unit for the words)

 40

(see unit for the words)

 41

1   Do / You / D'you smoke?
2   Have / To / We have to go.
3   Good / Girl / She's a good girl.
4   Next / Please / Next please.

 42

1 I'd like to introduce myself. My name's Jack and I'm here to talk about team-building.
2 I'd like to introduce myself. My name's May and I'm here to talk about finance.
3 I'd like to introduce myself. My name's Donna and I'm here to talk about sales.
4 I'd like to introduce myself. My name's Andy and I'm here to talk about personnel.
5 I'd like to introduce myself. My name's Shona and I'm here to talk about employment law.

43

1 I'd like to introduce myself. My name's Christian and I'm here to talk about technology.
2 I'd like to introduce myself. My name's Dan and I'm here to talk about training.
3 I'd like to introduce myself. My name's Anna and I'm here to talk about management.
4 I'd like to introduce myself. My name's Kirsti and I'm here to talk about marketing.
5 I'd like to introduce myself. My name's David and I'm here to talk about accountancy.

44

1 I'd like to introduce myself. My name's Sean and I'm here to talk about production.
2 I'd like to introduce myself. My name's Pete and I'm here to talk about giving effective presentations.
3 I'd like to introduce myself. My name's Collette and I'm here to talk about cross-cultural problems.
4 I'd like to introduce myself. My name's Bob and I'm here to talk about negotiating techniques.
5 I'd like to introduce myself. My name's Diana and I'm here to talk about effective emailing.

Module 7

Unit 1

45

Claire: I like your bag. Where's it from?
Brad: I picked it up at Heathrow Airport

while I was waiting for my flight.
Claire: They have so many shops there, don't they?
Brad: Yeah, and I had plenty of time. My flight was delayed by four hours.
Claire: Oh dear. So, what did you do? Just walk around the shops?
Brad: I got myself a book to read.
Claire: Anything interesting?
Brad: Yeah, it's called Snow; it's by this Turkish guy …
Claire: Orhan Pamuk.
Brad: That's the one. I guess you've heard of him?
Claire: Oh yes, I've read most of his novels. He won the Nobel Prize for Literature a couple of years ago.
Brad: Really? I didn't know that.
Claire: What do you think of the book?
Brad: I've only read the first few chapters. The story's quite slow, isn't it? But I like the style.
Claire: Actually, it's not an easy book to read. I recommend My Name is Red.
Brad: Is that another book of his?
Claire: Yes. I think you'd enjoy that more. It's a kind of murder mystery.
Brad: OK, thanks for the suggestion. I'll give it a try when I've finished this one.

Unit 2

 46

Marc: That reminds me of the last time I visited West Africa.
Claire: Oh yes?
Marc: When I got home, I felt incredibly ill.
Claire: That's a shame. What did you do?
Marc: I went to the hospital and spoke to a nurse. When I told her about my African trip, she moved me to a little room.
Claire: Really? What happened then?
Marc: When the doctor came to my room he put on a face mask and some gloves.
Claire: No!?!
Marc: And then he did some tests and told me to wait for two hours.
Claire: What did he say after that?
Marc: He told me that the tests showed I had a cold, not a tropical disease.
Claire: That was lucky. So, what did you do then?
Marc: I took some pills and went home.
Claire: That's funny.

Unit 3

 47

Marc: Of course, French food is the best in the world. We have more top class restaurants than anywhere else and …
Claire: Sorry to interrupt Marc, but …
Marc: Please go ahead, Claire.
Claire: I'm afraid I don't agree. There are excellent restaurants almost everywhere these days.
Marc: Perhaps. But the ones in France are

usually better.
Claire: You've travelled a lot Angie, what do you think?
Angie: Well, I think the best French restaurants probably are in France.
Marc: There you are, Angie agrees.
Angie: Well, actually Marc, to tell you the truth I don't really like French food as much as other national cuisines. I'm …
Marc: Really!?! But everyone …
Angie: Just a moment, let me finish what I was saying. I'm not keen on all those sauces. I prefer Italian – it's much simpler – and, of course, Chinese. What about you Claire?
Claire: I tend to agree with Angie. But I did live in Hong Kong for several years.
Marc: Sorry, but are you saying that Chinese food is better than French?
Claire: No, not better. It's just a question of preference.
Marc: Incredible!
Angie: I think we'll just have to agree to disagree on this one.
Claire: Yes, let's talk about something else.
Marc: That's a good idea. You are both interested in art, aren't you? Of course, Paris is the centre of the art world …
Angie & Claire: Marc!!

Unit 4

 48

Ashok: Have you been to India, Marc?
Marc: No, I haven't.
Ashok: What about you, Ingrid?
Ingrid: No, but I'd like to one day. It looks so exotic.
Marc: I have been to Asia several times. China's similar to India, isn't it?
Ashok: I'm sorry, I'm not with you.
Marc: I mean they're both huge countries with growing economies.
Ashok: Oh, now I see what you're saying. Yes, I suppose that's true.
Ingrid: What's the population of India?
Ashok: It's about a billion.
Marc: A billion?! That can't be right! Are you saying there are a million million people in India? No!
Ashok: No, actually a billion is a thousand million. Our population is about one point two billion.
Ingrid: Does everyone speak English?
Ashok: It's very important in business and government and universities. Our main language is actually Hindi but I think there are about 20 official languages and more than 1500 dialects.
Ingrid: Sorry, could you explain that again? Does everyone speak English?
Ashok: No, not everyone. Let me put it another way. We have lots of different languages around the country but, if you want to be successful in business, science or politics, you have to be able to speak

English as well.
Ingrid: So, in other words, English isn't a first language. Is that right?
Ashok: Yes, that's it.
Ingrid: OK, now I've got it. Thanks.

Module 8

Unit 1

 49

Well, the United Kingdom is actually made up of four countries: England, Scotland, Wales and Northern Ireland. … Did you know that the UK was the world's first industrialized country? It still has a large economy. I guess we mainly export manufactured goods, but I'm not sure. … We use the pound sterling. 100 pence makes a pound. The UK does not, of course, use the Euro. … The UK is also very ethnically diverse. We are well known for being quite a multicultural society. … I'm sure you know a lot of famous British musicians like the Beatles and the Rolling Stones, who were most famous in the 1960s. We also have a very rich literary heritage, with famous writers like William Shakespeare and Jane Austen. … It's also quite crowded: the population is over 61 million! … Of course, we have a world-famous royal family – you'll have heard of Queen Elizabeth II. … We have three main political parties: the Conservatives, the Labour Party and the Liberal Democrats. … The BBC is known around the world. And we also have commercial TV channels like ITV. … Oh, and we also have a huge number of newspapers in Britain! The most famous is probably The Times. There's also the Daily Telegraph, which is on the right politically, and The Guardian, which is on the left. Oh yes, and there's the tabloid press like The Sun and The Mirror.

Unit 2

 50

Good morning, ladies and gentlemen. The title of my workshop today is 'body language'. Did you know that many of the messages we give out come from non-verbal communication? We think we communicate when we speak, but much of our message is given through our body language. … What emotions and expressions does our face show? For example, are we smiling or frowning? Eye contact is another important area here. … And how about gestures? We can make all kinds of gestures, such as a 'thumbs up' sign to a friend before an important presentation or a nod of the head. … Often, our signals are unintentional, like touching your nose or your ear, or rubbing your eyes. You may even be giving out negative signals without meaning to. What happens if someone crosses her arms or legs, for example? This whole area is difficult because it is so easy to misinterpret signals. Maybe that person is just getting comfortable! What's more, these messages may be completely different in different cultures.

Unit 3

 51

1

Angie: Here's a good joke. Doctor Doctor, I have trouble sleeping at night. Don't worry. Just go to the side of the bed and you'll soon drop off.
Marc: I don't get it.
Angie: Well, drop off means fall asleep. It also means drop off the bed – and fall on the floor.
Marc: Oh, I see.
Angie: It's a play on words.
Marc: Well, it's not that funny.

2

Ashok: What's wrong?
Brad: Well, I was talking to the guys down in the computer section and they were laughing all the time. I just couldn't see what was so funny.
Ashok: Oh don't worry. It's just a little joke that people in their group understand, but outsiders don't. It's got something to do with their boss's surname. If you say it fast, it means 'silly person'.
Brad: Is that all it is? Oh OK, I understand now.

3

Angie: I just pretended to laugh, but actually I didn't understand the end.
Claire: I know what you mean. It's horrible – you understand the whole joke, but just not the last line.

4

Ingrid: I hate those people in sales. They're always making clever remarks and telling jokes. But actually, they can really upset people.
Angie: You're right. They're very clever things they say, but they can definitely hurt or annoy people.

5

Ingrid: I was watching a TV show last night and every time Joey said 'Forgive me', the audience just fell about laughing. Why?
Brad: Don't worry. It's just a little joke that runs through every show. The audience just expect to laugh at it and they do. You have to watch the show regularly to find it funny.

Unit 4

 52

You know, when I first went to Spain, it was difficult. One day, I'd arranged to meet Juan, my Spanish business contact, in the bar at 8.30. Well, being prompt, I arrived at 8.28. He didn't arrive. I waited until 8.45. No sign of him. I called his mobile. He said

he was 'on his way'. It was now 9.05 and I was really beginning to get angry. Then suddenly, I remembered a cultural training course I had taken before the trip. The trainer had said that many people in Spain have a more laid-back attitude to time and punctuality. So I had another gin and tonic and took it easy. When Juan finally arrived I was feeling relaxed and happy, and the evening turned out to be a great success.

Module 9

Unit 1

 53

(see unit for the words)

 54

1 My favourite film is Notting Hill. It's a nice love story and Julia Roberts and Hugh Grant are such fun together.
2 My favourite movie is The Blair Witch Project. I know it was just a film but I was really, really frightened.
3 My all-time favourite film is Star Wars. I love films about the future. Have you seen 2001: A Space Odyssey?
4 My favourite film is Pride and Prejudice. Jane Austen is so popular nowadays. The old-fashioned dresses are gorgeous.
5 Don't you just love the James Bond films? I loved Goldfinger, it was so exciting – I was totally gripped!
6 I grew up watching Disney movies. I absolutely love The Lion King. Cartoons aren't just for children, you know!
7 I love Mamma Mia. Have you seen it at the cinema? I went with my friend and we just couldn't stop singing along.
8 My favourite film is Saving Private Ryan. Tom Hanks is brilliant as the army captain who goes looking for a missing soldier.

 55

Angie: What do you think of this one, Marc? Amazing, isn't it!
Marc: Hmm, I'm not sure – I think Dali's just too weird for my taste.
Angie: Come on, at least it's interesting – not like Monet and the other impressionists. They're so boring.
Marc: Do you really think so? I love the French impressionists, the way they interpret nature.
Angie: Maybe, but they're not really my style. Oh, but here's one thing I know neither of us like …
Marc: Ah yes, modern art! No, I'm not a big fan at all – far too abstract for my liking.
Angie: Yes, I agree with you on that.

 56

Claire: Have you read Enduring Love? I've just started it. Chapter 1 is amazing.
Ingrid: Enduring Love? No. Who's the

author?
Claire: Er, Ian Rankin … I mean, Ian McEwan. He won the Booker Prize for his book Amsterdam. Have you read anything by him?
Ingrid: McEwan? I'm afraid not. What's the book like?
Claire: Oh, I'm absolutely loving it.
Ingrid: Why?
Claire: It's just completely absorbing. I just can't put it down.

Unit 2

 57

1

Marc: Did you see the match last night?
Ingrid: What match?
Marc: Oh, nothing. I was talking about the European Cup. Obviously you don't follow football.
Ingrid: No, I don't.
Marc: Do you follow any sports?
Ingrid: Tennis is my thing.
Marc: Tennis? Oh, I used to play too. I love watching Wimbledon.

2

Marc: Did you see the match last night?
Ashok: Yes – it was amazing, wasn't it? But the referee should have given that penalty in the last minute.
Marc: No way. It was never a penalty.
Ashok: It was clearly a handball. So, who do you think will win the cup?
Marc: Germany. And you?
Ashok: Italy. Who do you support?
Marc: France of course. Oh, and I'm a fan of Marseilles.

 58

1 Chelsea drew last night, after extra time – despite going two goals up in the first half.
2 He skidded on the bend and nearly came off the track. The Ferrari team were worried, but he still won the race.
3 She was running fast off the final bend but then she hit the last hurdle – and just missed out on the record.
4 It was a gripping final. But at deuce in the first game of the third set, he suddenly got injured and had to stop playing.
5 Well, I suppose you could say it's a kind of martial art, you know, from the Far East. It's a bit like judo, I guess.
6 What a thrilling climax it was to the season. The French took the victory, thanks to a brilliant try and drop-goal.
7 He hasn't managed to play eighteen holes all year, but on his first shot, can you believe it … he got a hole in one!
8 He was so great at the Olympics. We even joke about him being like a fish in the pool. He won the backstroke final.

Unit 3

 59

Good evening. The headlines tonight on Tuesday March 1st … A German car tycoon is arrested in Stuttgart … Scientists announce new evidence in the fight against climate change … Unions back down in trade dispute in France – a strike has been avoided … And in Colombia, five hostages are freed amidst jungle drama … Also on tonight's programme, the global credit crunch: is there a light at the end of the tunnel? … And finally, the weather where you are.

 60

Fritz Schwarz, the German car tycoon, has been arrested in Stuttgart on charges of fraud and tax evasion. Schwarz is accused of cheating the German government out of 100,000 Euros. He is currently being held in custody, and is expected to stand trial next month.

Does global warming really exist? Scientists have announced new evidence in the fight against climate change. They have recorded higher temperatures around the world, and claim the data finally offers proof that the planet is indeed hotting up.

The unions have finally backed down in the long-running trade dispute in France. After lengthy negotiations with the management, it looks like another round of strikes has been avoided.

In Colombia, five French hostages were freed at the weekend. The five had been kidnapped by rebel forces, and were feared dead. They are expected to join their families in Paris shortly in what is sure to be an emotional reunion.

Also on tonight's programme, the global credit crunch. Our finance correspondent Mark Short asks: is there light at the end of the tunnel? After a number of high-profile bankruptcies, and thousands of redundancies, it seems that the worst is over. The markets are starting to rally and the downturn appears to be a thing of the past.

And finally, the local weather forecast for the next twenty-four hours. More stormy weather is expected tonight, with the promise of sunny spells tomorrow. The outlook for next week is good.

Unit 4

 61

1

Salesperson: You really need to consider using the latest technology when delivering training. Your best option is to buy an interactive whiteboard.
Ashok: Why should we spend the whole of our budget on just one gadget?

Salesperson: Well, it's a very powerful training tool. It will help to keep your trainers and your training programme up to speed with your competitors.
Ashok: We have a data projector and a laptop. I think that's probably enough. Besides, it's just too expensive.
Salesperson: I know it's not cheap, but don't you think it's wise to invest in equipment? OK, let me see, perhaps I can interest you in a low-cost alternative? Why don't you get one of these? It's a portable model and half the price.
Ashok: Now you're talking.

2

Robert: It's a fantastic opportunity, darling, a one-off.
Claire: It's a great opportunity for **you**, Robert. What am I supposed to do – give up my job?
Robert: There'll be jobs in China.
Claire: That's ridiculous. I would have to learn a whole new language.
Robert: I doubt it. Anyway, the money is great. Come on. You have to admit that my salary can support us both.
Claire: Sure. But it would be hard on the kids. They'd have to interrupt their schooling. You'll never convince me.
Robert: Just think about it. It's not every day this kind of promotion comes up.

3

Ingrid: It's ten past nine. The meeting is starting late.
Brad: I think Marc's train has been delayed. It's only ten minutes.
Ingrid: Why didn't he come the night before? It's much safer. It's really not acceptable to start late.
Brad: Ingrid. Wouldn't you agree that in some cultures it's perfectly normal to start a meeting five or even ten minutes late?
Ingrid: Well, 9 o'clock means 9 o'clock where I come from. Besides, I've got other things to do.
Brad: Yes, but come on. A late train is completely beyond anyone's control.
Ingrid: OK, maybe you're right, but at the end of the day, late is late.

 62

1

Ashok: I think it's a disgrace that the bosses drive these gas-guzzlers. It's obvious that cars are one of the major causes of pollution.
Marc: Oh, rubbish. Next you'll be telling us that we shouldn't fly. Look, global warming cannot be blamed on just one thing. What do you think, Claire?
Claire: I don't have an opinion one way or another. I think now would be a good time to change the subject.

2

Ingrid: You're joking. Are you telling me that you don't have an ID card? What

happens when you have to prove who you are?
Claire: Easy. I just show my driver's licence. Or my passport.
Ingrid: A-ha. And what if I don't drive? Or I don't travel?
Claire: Well, I would take in a letter with my address on it …
Ingrid: Oh for goodness sake, no wonder there's so much identity fraud. How easy is it to get a letter like that? ID cards prove who you are. And they help in the prevention of fraud and terrorism.
Claire: Well, I've lived all my life without an ID card. Do you really think I want to give my details to a giant database?
Brad: Woah – guys, calm down a bit. Look, let's just say that some countries do and some countries don't. That's just the way it is. Now how about we just drop it? Let me get you both a drink and let's change the topic. I think it's better not to talk about something we really can't change anyway. Don't you agree?

3

Marc: Mind if I smoke?
Ingrid: Well actually, it's a no smoking building. Best do it outside.
Marc: Fine. You know, I can't wait to go home. All this 'You can't smoke here' nonsense. People telling me what I can and can't do …
Ingrid: Well actually, it makes perfect sense. When others smoke, the people around them have to smoke – passively.
Marc: Yes, but they could just stay at home. I mean, why go out to a bar in the first place? Isn't a bar where people smoke and drink? Right, Claire?
Claire: I'd prefer not to say. It's a tricky one. I think we should talk about something else.

4

Marc: I don't believe it. I asked a colleague if she would burn me the latest Madonna album. She actually said no!
Claire: She's right. Copying music for friends is the same as stealing royalties from the artist.
Marc: As if Madonna's poor! If there's music up on the internet, who owns it?
Claire: Well, even if it's on the internet, copyright law still applies.
Marc: Oh come on. Everyone does it. And music is digital nowadays – it's not something on a disc anyway. That's what the Web is all about, isn't it? File sharing? Ashok?
Ashok: I, er, it's difficult to say. It's quite a controversial topic. I think it's better not to talk about it right now. I mean, we're supposed to be enjoying ourselves.

Grammar focus tables

Module 5 Unit 1 – adjectives, comparatives and superlatives

FORM

Adjective	Comparative	Superlative	Notes
fast	faster **than**	the fast**est**	adjective has one syllable
big	big**ger than**	the big**gest**	adjective ends in a vowel and a consonant; double the final consonant
easy	eas**ier than**	the eas**iest**	adjective ends in -y: change the 'y' to 'i'
beautiful	**more** beautiful **than**	the **most** beautiful	adjective has two or more syllables
good	**better than**	the **best**	irregular
bad	**worse than**	the **worst**	irregular

USE

1 We use <u>adjectives</u> to describe people, places and things: *I have a slim mobile phone*.
2 We use the <u>comparative</u> form to compare two things: *New York City is bigger than Washington*.
3 We use the <u>superlative</u> when we compare more than two things: *Russia is the biggest country in the world*.

Module 5 Unit 2 – present tenses

<u>Present simple</u> FORM I / You / We / They **live** in Madrid. (+) I **don't live** in Barcelona. (-) **Do** you live in London? (?) He / She / It **lives** in Peru. (+) He **doesn't live** in Mexico. (-) **Does** she live in Brazil? (?)	USE We use this tense to speak about: 1) how often we do things: *I never speak German*. 2) permanent things and facts: *I live here*.
<u>Present continuous</u> FORM **I'm staying** at the Grand Hotel. (+) I'm / You're / He's / She's / We're / They're staying at the Ritz. **He's not staying** at the Holiday Inn. (-) I'm / You're / He's / She's / We're / They're not staying at the Plaza. **Are you staying** at the Hilton? (?) Am I / Are you / Is he / Is she / Are we / Are they staying at the Mercure?	USE We use this tense to speak about: 1) projects we are currently involved in: *I'm working in Cuba for a few weeks*. 2) situations which are temporary: *This month, we're closing early on Fridays for staff training*. 3) actions happening at the moment of speaking: *I'm just emailing it over now*.

Module 5 Unit 2 – modal verbs

FORM	All modal verbs have the same form: Subject + modal verb + verb (infinitive)

USE

Can	Must / Have to	Should	Mustn't / Can't	Don't have to
We use *can* to: - speak about possibility: *I can see you on Sunday afternoon.* - speak about ability: *I can play golf pretty well.* - ask for permission: *Can we use this seminar room?*	We use *must* and *have to* to: - speak about obligation: *You have to have a visa to go there.* - give strong advice: *You must stop smoking.*	We use *should* to: - speak about less strong obligation: *We should go now.* - give advice: *You should complete that form.*	We use *mustn't* and *can't* to: - talk about prohibition: *You really mustn't go there.* *We can't stay here long.*	We use *don't have to* to: - say that something isn't necessary: *If you take the fast train, you don't have to travel overnight.*

Other common modals are *may* and *might*: *She may join us later.* / *He might leave early.*

Module 5 Unit 3 – past simple and present perfect

Past simple	USE
FORM I / You / He / She / We / They **opened** the file. (+) I **didn't open** the file. (-) **Did** you open the file? (?) I / You / He / She / We / They **went** there. (+) I **didn't go** there. (-) **Did** you go there? (?) Verbs are either regular or irregular. Regular verbs add -ed or -d: *I opened the file / He signed the contract / She arrived late.* Irregular verbs need to be learnt as individual items: *I **went** there / They **paid** me / I **saw** him.*	We use this tense when we specify a time in the past. Typical 'time markers' (expressions which are often used with a particular tense) are: *ago (eg five years ago) / yesterday / last year / when I was at … (eg school).* Sometimes we understand the time marker, even if we don't say it: *She left.* (The speaker means: she left after the meeting.)
Present perfect	USE
FORM I / You / We / They **have seen** her. (+) Subject + *have* is usually contracted to I've, you've, etc. He / She / It **has seen** her. (+) Subject + *has* is usually contracted to he's, she's, etc. I **haven't met** the CEO. / She **hasn't arrived** yet. (-) **Have you seen** her? **Has he seen** them? (?) Verbs are either regular or irregular. Regular verbs add -ed or -d: *We have look**ed** at the figures / She hasn't arrived yet.* Irregular verbs need to be learnt as individual items: *They have **seen** her / He has **gone** home / I haven't **met** the CEO.*	We use this tense to talk about: - an action which started in the past and continues until now: *I've lived here since 2002.* - a past action which affects the present: *I've broken my leg* (past), *so I cannot walk* (now) - past experiences, where the specific time is not important: *Have you seen ET?* Typical 'time markers' (expressions which are often used with a particular tense) are: *so far / yet / already / up to now / this week / this month.* Note the different uses of *for* and *since*: - *for* shows a length of time: *I've lived here for 10 years.* - *since* shows a starting point: *I've lived here since 2002.*

Module 5 Unit 4 – future forms

Going to	Will
FORM Subject + am/are/is (am not/aren't/isn't) + going to + verb (infinitive)	FORM Subject + will (won't) + verb (infinitive)
USE When we talk about plans or intentions, or to make predictions: *She's going to buy more shares this week.* *I think you're going to like this.*	USE To make predictions or instant decisions: *I think Liverpool will win.* *I'll call them.*
Present continuous	Present simple
FORM See Module 5 Unit 2 grammar focus table (present tenses)	FORM See Module 5 Unit 2 grammar focus table (present tenses)
USE When we talk about fixed arrangements: *We're meeting at 10am.*	USE When we talk about schedules or timetables: *Your flight leaves at 10 tonight.*

Module 5 Unit 4 – conditionals

Conditional type 0	Conditional type 1	Conditional type 2
FORM present simple + present simple	FORM present simple + will (/won't)	FORM past simple + would (/wouldn't)
USE For general truths or things that always happen: *If he **has** too much work, he **gets** stressed.* *When I **turn** it on, I **hear** a strange sound.*	USE When talking about possible or probable future events, and often used for making decisions: *If we **follow** their advice, we'**ll avoid** the problem.* *If you **decide** to work with us, you **won't regret** it.*	USE When considering impossible or improbable situations in the future: *If I **owned** the company, I'**d do** things differently.* *If she **joined** our main rival, I **would be** really unhappy.*

Answer key

Module 1

Unit 1

2a.
They do not know each other very well.

2b.

1	a	3	b	5	a
2	b	4	a	6	b

4.

1	in	3	ago	5	on
2	from, to	4	for	6	since

6.

1	moved	3	to graduate	5	started
2	joined	4	doing	6	travel

Unit 2

1.

1	b	3	c	5	e	7	a
2	f	4	g	6	h	8	d

2a.
1 Where are you from?
2 What do you do?
3 Who do you work for?
4 How long have you been in your job?
5 When did you join the company?
6 Where are you based?
7 Why did you join your company?
8 How many people work in your department?

3a.
They are in India.

3b.

1	a, b	3	a, c
2	b	4	a

3c.
They turn the question around when talking about visiting the US, visiting Europe and being married.

4a.
1 Where **do** you come from?
2 How **long** have you lived in Berlin?
3 **Are you** married?
4 **Do you have any** children?
5 Where **did** you go on holiday last year?
6 **Have you got** your new car yet?

4b.

a	5	c	1	e	6
b	4	d	3	f	2

Unit 3

1.
Answer 2 is better because it gives more information and doesn't assume that the listener knows the company.

2.

1	e	3	b	5	d	7	h
2	g	4	c	6	a	8	f

3a.
Markets: the US and Canada
Workforce: Ashok and 16 programmers in India, Ashok's partner and two salespeople in the US
Turnover: last year about US$2 million
Profit: a little over US$200,000
Number of clients: about 50

3b.
Brad misunderstands the number of programmers in Ashok's company. Ashok explains that the number is 'one six' (16) and not 'six zero' (60).

5a.

1	d	5	c/g
2	f	6	h/b
3	b /h	7	e
4	a	8	g/c

5b.
1 won, contract
2 set up, subsidiary
3 hire/recruit, staff
4 increase, budget
5 lay, people off
6 made, contingency plans
7 lose, contracts

6a.

1	–	4	+	7	+ +	10	+ +
2	+	5	+	8	–		
3	– –	6	– –	9	+		

Unit 4

1a.

1	c	2	a	3	b

1b.
The greetings used in the dialogues are:
How do you do? / Morning / Good morning / Hello / Pleased to meet you

2a.
Dialogue 1: a, e, c, d, b
Dialogue 2: a, f, d, e, c, b, g
The first dialogue is more formal.

3.

1	Great	5	Fine
2	Very well	6	Not great
3	Good	7	Not too good
4	Pretty good	8	Terrible

4a.
1 catch you tomorrow
2 Good night
3 you in the morning
4 lovely to see you again
5 You too
6 Bye
7 Take care
8 nice meeting you
9 Thank you again
10 Goodbye.
11 a safe journey

4b.
Greeting a = Goodbye 3
Greeting b = Goodbye 1
Greeting c = Goodbye 2

Module 2

Unit 1

1.
Key to scores:
10 points or more: Congratulations! You have a good work-life balance!
5–9: Not bad. You could make some improvements to your lifestyle.
4 or less: It's time to change your lifestyle. Why not take up a new hobby?

2b.
do: yoga / gardening / tai chi / pilates / sport
play: computer games / cards / the guitar / chess / squash
go: parachuting / scuba diving / fishing / swimming / jogging

3a.

1	Ingrid	3	Ashok
2	Angie	4	Brad

3b.
1 a window seat on the plane
2 the traffic jams
3 because she hates flying
4 the next time he's in London

Unit 2

1.

1	continent	3	county	5	town
2	country	4	city	6	village

2a.
Subjects mentioned: statues, castles, museums, palaces (but <u>not</u> cinemas, parks, zoos or restaurants)

2b.
Royal Mile _4_
Edinburgh Castle _3_
Princes Street _1_
Scott's Monument _2_
Holyrood Palace _6_
Royal Museum of Scotland _5_

2c.
1 You must visit Princes Street.
2 Don't miss the Royal Mile.
3 I'd recommend visiting the Royal Museum.
4 You should see the famous statue.

3a.

1	fair	4	souvenir
2	population	5	ruins
3	speciality	6	district

4a.

1	Japan	3	Germany
2	China	4	UK

4b.
Speaker 1: best time to visit, temples, trains, currency
Speaker 2: the largest town, festivals
Speaker 3: local speciality
Speaker 4: souvenirs

Unit 3

1.
Vegetables: peppers / mushroom / broccoli / lettuce / potato
Fruit: cherry / strawberry / mango / peach / pineapple
Meat and poultry: pork / lamb / chicken / turkey / beef
Fish and seafood: salmon / cod / prawns / mussels / tuna

2a.
Brad has the healthier diet.

2b.
1 F   2 F   3 T   4 T

3a.
coffee   5   starter   2
dessert   4   main course   3
aperitif   1

4a.
1 drink   4 wine
2 juice   5 beer
3 water

4b.
1 e   3 g   5 a   7 b
2 f   4 c   6 d

Unit 4

1a.
Positive: challenging, glamorous, rewarding
Negative: demanding, repetitive, stressful

1b.
1 Claire   5 Ashok
2 Ashok   6 Claire
3 Ingrid   7 Marc
4 Marc   8 Ingrid

2a.
1 Chief Executive Officer
2 Payroll clerk
3 Finance director
4 Head of IT
5 Research and Development manager

2b.
1 h   3 a   5 c   7 g
2 f   4 d   6 b   8 e

3a.
1 personal assistant
2 careers adviser
3 Web designer
4 call centre assistant

Module 3

Unit 1

2.
1 love   5 OK, nothing
2 a lot, really   6 don't like
3 quite   7 don't like
4 a little   8 hate

4a.
Angie likes travelling the most.

4b.
1 a   2 c   3 b   4 a

5.
1 We could go
2 I'd prefer
3 Do you like
4 Which would you prefer
5 It depends
6 I'd definitely prefer
7 Me too

6.
1 d   3 e   5 c
2 b   4 a

Polite language: I'm afraid … / I'm sorry, but … / I prefer …

Unit 2

2.
a 1   c 3   e 5
b 6   d 2   f 4

3a.
1 would   2 Do   3 Do   4 Do

3b.
a 3   b 4   c 2   d 1

4a.
1 b   2 a   3 b

4b.
1, 3 and 5 are all appropriate. (The other three would be considered rude.)

5a.
They are talking about having dinner at Claire's house. Claire, Ingrid and Angie Wong-Smith are going to be there.

5b.
1 b   3 b   5 c
2 c   4 a   6 b

Unit 3

2a.
2 and 4 sound more formal but all the phrases are polite.

2b.
1 lost my passport
2 upset my colleague
3 close down this program

2c.
a 2   b 3   c 1

2d.
1 a   2 b   3 c   4 b

4a.
a 3   b 1   c 4   d 2

4b.
a She recommends a bus tour. It is a good way for first-time visitors to see the most famous places.
b She recommends the Novotel. It's close to the centre of the city and he might get a discount if he books early.
c She recommends something from the Ampelmann Shop. The Ampelmann (the little traffic light man) is a modern symbol of the city.
d She recommends an exclusive place in the east of the city. It is run by her friend.

4c.
1   a Can you recommend a reasonably priced one?
    b I suggest you book a room at the Novotel.
2   a What do you think I should do?
    b You should take a bus tour.
3   a What's a typical souvenir from Berlin?
    b If I were you, I would get them something from the Ampelmann Shop in Potsdamer Platz.

5.
1 b, iv   2 c, ii   3 a, iii   4 d, i

Unit 4

2a.
They are talking about the European Union. Angie finds it useful to hear the opinions of Europeans on the subject.

2b.
1 positive   3 negative
2 negative   4 positive

2c.
Asking for opinions: <u>What do you think about …?</u> / Do you think …? / What's your opinion on …? / How do you see it?

Giving opinions: <u>I think …</u> / In my opinion, … / <u>From my point of view, …</u> / <u>It seems to me that …</u> / <u>I'm sure that …</u> / <u>I'm convinced that …</u>

Agreeing: Yes, that's right. / I agree with you. / <u>I completely agree.</u> / Absolutely.

Disagreeing: I don't agree. / I'm sorry, I can't agree. / I see what you mean, but … / I'm sorry, but surely that's not right.

(The underlined phrases are those used by Marc and Angie.)

3.
(Most positive first) a brilliant, a very good, a good, an interesting, quite an interesting, a poor, a bad, a terrible

4.
1 a=A, b=DD, c=TD
2 a=TD, b=DD, c=A
3 a=A, b=TD, c=DD

Module 4

Unit 1

1a.
1 bar   2 pub   3 coffee shop

2a.
They decide to go a traditional English pub

because it is a quiet place where they can talk (about Marc's proposal).

2b.
1 T
2 F (He thinks it doesn't have very much atmosphere)
3 F (They go to the bar to order their drinks but don't sit there)
4 T
5 T
6 F (Ingrid decides to buy some nibbles/ pork scratchings)

2c.
1 listen   3 sit   5 order
2 have   4 find   6 get

2d.
Ingrid ordered a coffee because she does not drink alcohol.
1 c   2 a   3 b

3.
1 f   3 b   5 d
2 c   4 a   6 e

Unit 2
2.
1 fork   8 soup spoon
2 wine glass   9 napkin
3 saucer   10 tea spoon
4 dessert spoon   11 cup
5 plate   12 butter knife
6 water glass   13 knife
7 soup bowl   14 side plate

3a.
1 a   2 b   3 b   4 a

3b.
1 Host   3 Guest 5 Host
2 Host   4 Host   6 Guest

3c.
a 5   b 6   c 1   d 2

4a.
1 C   3 P   5 P   7 C   9 P
2 C   4 P   6 P   8 C   10 C

5a.
1 d   2 e   3 a   4 c   5 b

5b.
1 c   2 a

Unit 3
1.
This depends on your own experience, but generally trade fairs might include demonstrations of new products and free product samples. The other five activities can happen at both events.

2a.
1 f   3 a   5 b
2 c   4 e   6 d

2b.
The future of personnel management. John Barrymore is giving the talk.

2c.
1 T   3 T   5 T
2 T   4 F   6 F

3a.
Printed materials: brochure, leaflet, flyer, handout
Other types of material: giveaway, freebie, sample, tester

4a.
a 1   c 8   e 6   g 4
b 2   d 3   f 5   h 7

5.
1 Have you had a good time?
2 Have you learnt anything useful?
3 What was the most interesting session?
4 Did you make any useful contacts?
5 Are you going again next year?

Unit 4
2.
1 help   3 have   5 put   7 let
2 see   4 sign   6 call   8 take

3a.
1 office   4 a bottle of wine
2 a glass of water   5 the sitting room
3 more modern   6 white wine

3b.
1 c, j   3 b, e   5 d, f
2 h, i   4 a, g

4a.
1 on time   3 too late
2 late   4 in time

4b.
The acceptable excuses are 1, 4, 5, 6 and 8 (depending on how they are expressed).

5.
1 How was your journey?
2 Oh dear, why was that?
3 Is this your first time here?
4 When were you here before?
5 How long are you staying?
6 Where are you staying?
7 How are things where you are?

Module 5

Unit 1
Communication breakdown!
The question 'What's somewhere/someone/ something like?' is usually answered with an adjective. 'Do you like?' is a completely different question, and relates to preference and personal taste.

1.
Incorrect sentences:
1 Madrid is the same ~~than~~ as Barcelona.
2 It is the most beautiful city ~~of~~ in the world.

4 It's a ~~car blue~~ blue car.
5 The ~~economical~~ economic situation is very bad.
7 This question is ~~more easy~~ easier than that one.
8 This is the ~~worstest~~ worst company in the world.

3a.
1 light, portable
2 historic, busy
3 dark-haired, pretty
4 handsome, blond
5 automatic, fast
6 peaceful, green

3b.
1 ancient   2 ugly   3 lazy   4 noisy

3c.
1 inaccurate   4 unwise
2 unreliable   5 impatient
3 unsympathetic   6 intolerant

5a.
New York City 2   London   3
Berlin   X   Tokyo   5
Paris   4   Barcelona   1

5b.
1 slimmer/slimmest
2 trendier/trendiest
3 cheaper/cheapest
4 more effective/most effective
5 better/best
6 worse/worst

5c.
1 New York is much more exciting than anywhere else.
2 London is so much busier than Paris.
3 London is more crowded than most capital cities.
4 London is dirtier than most capital cities.
5 It is much more expensive than most other places.
6 Paris is more romantic than anywhere else I know.

Unit 2
Communication breakdown!
The second speaker has used the wrong present tense. The present continuous 'I'm working for IBM' means that his job is temporary, and it will finish soon. However, he actually wants to say that this is his permanent job, so he should use the present simple 'I work for IBM', instead.

1.
Incorrect sentences:
1 I ~~am~~ work for Metro.
3 He likes Rome.
4 ~~I'm usually going~~ I usually go there by underground.
5 I ~~work rarely~~ rarely work at this factory.
6 ~~I'm not understanding~~ I don't understand your accent.
8 ~~Your boss wants~~ Does your boss want to join us?

3.

1	am staying	5	likes
2	are working	6	I usually go
3	Does	7	Do
4	am working	8	Does

Communication breakdown!
The opposite of 'must' (obligation) is 'don't have to' (no obligation). However, the second speaker believes the opposite of 'must' is 'mustn't' (which actually means prohibition). So here it sounds like something is stopping him from flying after four o' clock!

5.
1 I cannot ~~to~~ speak German.
2 We must ~~to~~ go now.
3 I ~~don't can~~ can't/don't understand you.
4 He ~~don't~~ doesn't have to work at night.
5 We ~~mustn't~~ don't have to pay VAT – it's optional.
6 You shouldn't ~~to~~ smoke.
7 You ~~mustn't~~ don't have to pay by cash, you can pay by credit card
8 ~~Have you~~ Do you have to work every day?

7.

1	must	5	cannot
2	don't have	6	doesn't have to
3	can't	7	don't have to
4	must	8	shouldn't

Unit 3
Communication breakdown!
The first speaker is asking a question about the future: 'How long are you here for?' She is expecting the answer 'until Friday'. However, the second speaker has understood the question as 'How long **have you been** here for?', so he answers 'For three minutes' – in other words, he arrived three minutes ago.

1.
Incorrect sentences:
1 ~~I'm living~~ I've lived here for three years.
2 ~~I've lived~~ I lived here three years ago.
3 I ~~didn't finish~~ haven't finished the report yet.
5 I have lived here ~~since~~ for three years.
6 I ~~have spoken~~ spoke to Ashok yesterday.
7 I ~~am~~ have been here since Friday.
8 I've ~~gone to~~ been to Rhodes six times.

3a.
1 lived
2 designed, worked
3 did you start, joined
4 went, dropped out
5 got, didn't like

3b.

a	5	c	1	e	2
b	4	d	6	f	3

4a.

sent	talked	read	lived
received	been	tried	arrived
written	taken	left	come

4b.
1 d   2 a   3 b   4 c

5a.

1	since	3	up to now
2	four days ago	4	yet

5b.

1	worked	4	has finished
2	Have, attended	5	hasn't made
3	got		

Unit 4
Communication breakdown!
The second speaker uses the 'will' future form too much. To sound more natural, the speaker needs to use a range of future forms, such as 'going to', the present continuous and the present simple.

1.
Incorrect sentences:
1 ~~I present~~ I'm presenting / I'm going to present at a conference next month.
4 I **will** do it now.
5 I think United ~~are winning~~ will win / are going to win the cup next season.

3a.

1	FA or PI	3	ST	5	PR
2	FA	4	ID	6	PI

3b.
1 'll get (will get) / 're going to get (are going to get)
2 'm going to learn (am going to learn)
3 'm not going to repeat (am not going to repeat) / won't repeat (will not repeat)
4 'm meeting (am meeting)
5 leaves
6 'll let (will let)

3c.
The following future forms should be used for each question:
1 will (or going to)
2 present continuous
3 going to
4 present simple
5 will

Communication breakdown!
The listener does not realize that this question is 'hypothetical' (based on possible events, not actual ones). They think that 'lost' is talking about a past action, rather than speculating about future possibilities.

4.
1 When shares are cheap, ~~we'd~~ we buy / we'll buy a lot of them.
2 If we sell our shares, ~~we'd~~ we / we'll lose a lot of money!
3 If we sold our shares, ~~we'll~~ we'd lose millions.

6a.

1	a P	2	a P	3	a A	4	a A/P
	b I		b I		b I		b I

6b.

1	had	4	didn't have
2	don't hurry	5	would you choose
3	's/is	6	would be

Module 6
Unit 1
1b.

Contractions	6	Slang	5
Accent	4	Speed	1
Idioms	3	Vocabulary	2

1c.
1 the 23rd
2 tort
3 I wouldn't touch it with a bargepole (= I wouldn't go anywhere near it)
4 Scotland
5 have a gander (= have a quick look)
6 wouldn't've

3a.
Sandra is a better listener than John because:
- she checks information
- she asks him to repeat anything that isn't clear
- she corrects him when he makes a mistake.

3b.
1 Could you say that a little slower?
2 Could you repeat that please?

4a.
Best: Listener 2; Worst: Listener 1

4b.
Model answer:
An active listener gives the speaker their full and undivided attention. They also show their understanding through eye contact, nodding and smiling. They sometimes repeat some of the speaker's words, or check they have understood by rephrasing.

5a.
Key to scores:
19–24 points: excellent listener!
13–18 points: good listener
7–12 points: room for improvement
0–6 points: you need to work hard to improve your listening skills

Unit 2
2.
1 d   2 b   3 a   4 c   5 e

4.
1 The effects of the credit crunch.
2 Because a report about it was in the newspapers last week.
3 Marc. Because the report did not consider the human cost of the credit crunch.
4 Marc and Claire.
5 Claire and Angie.
6 Ashok. Because more companies started sourcing their IT services from India.

5.

1	O	3	F	5	F
2	O	4	F		

6.

1	c	3	a	5	d
2	b	4	e		

7a.

1	had been	4	had been
2	had cancelled	5	had doubled
3	was		

Unit 3

1a.

a

1	d	2	c	3	a	4	b

b

i   marc dot gisset at central dash(/hyphen) international dot fr

ii   aj underscore patel at iol dot tech dot co dot in

iii   bj dot ruby at greatbear dash(/hyphen) productions dot com

1b.

1   Claire has left **her new business cards** in her hotel room.

2   The information is out of date because **the bank she works for has been taken over.**

3   **Ashok** writes the new contact details on Claire's old card.

4   Claire gives Ashok her **personal mobile phone number.**

1c.

Windman Brothers Bank (**change to BGB Bank**)

Tel: 020 477 4730 (**change to 020 472 00349**)

Email: cthanet.hr@windmanbros.co.uk (**change to claire.thanet@bgbbank.com**) (**and add personal mobile number 0734 204 9090**)

2a.

1	150	3	3G	5	30
2	3.5	4	12	6	3

3a.

The restaurant is marked by a cross on the map.

3c.

1	out	4	turning
2	turn	5	miss
3	end	6	side

7	in front of	11	behind
8	follow	12	next
9	corner	13	on
10	straight	14	with

Unit 4

1a.

a	7	c	6	e	2	g	5
b	1	d	4	f	3		

1b.

1	/ɔː/ - /ɜː/	3	/æ/ - /e/
2	/l/ - /r/	4	/p/ - /b/

2.

ad<u>ver</u>tisement   pho<u>to</u>graphy

de<u>vel</u>opment   a<u>gen</u>da

<u>plen</u>ary   <u>in</u>teresting

<u>prod</u>uct   misunder<u>stan</u>ding

<u>rec</u>ord   re<u>cord</u>

<u>trans</u>fer   trans<u>fer</u>

3.

1   Where are you from? ↗

2   I wonder if you can help me? ↗

3   Excuse me, could you tell me how to get to the bus station? ↗

4   What time does the next session begin? ↗

4.

1	a	2	b	3	b

5.

1	weak	2	strong	3	weak

6.

1   'Do you' sounds like /dʒə/.

2   In 'have to', the /v/ becomes /f/.

3   The /d/ sound at the end of the word 'good' changes to a /g/ sound.

4   The /t/ sound at the end of the word 'next' disappears.

7.

Group 1: Australia, USA, South Africa, Caribbean, Canada

Group 2: Mexico, Japan, Russia, Finland, India

Group 3: Scotland, Ireland, Wales, England-London, England-Liverpool

Module 7

Unit 1

2a.

Not appropriate: 2, 6, 8, 9, 10

3a.

Topics mentioned: 2, 4, 5

Common topic: 4

3b.

1	a	2	b	3	a	4	b

4a.

1	don't they	2	isn't it

4b.

1	isn't it	4	isn't she
2	aren't you	5	don't they
3	hasn't it	6	won't it

5a.

1	When	4	Suddenly
2	At first	5	Then
3	but	6	So

Unit 2

1.

1, 3, 4 and 6.

2a.

Oh yes?	No!?!
That's a shame	That was lucky
Really?	That's funny

2b.

1   Oh yes? / Uh-huh? / Really? / Right / Go on / I see

2   That's funny / No!?! / That's incredible! / Is that so? (Note: 'Really?' could also go in this section.)

3   That's good news / That was lucky / That's great

4   That's a shame / How awful / Oh dear

2c.

Suggested answers:

1	That's good news.	4	Oh dear.
2	That was lucky.	5	No!?!
3	Oh yes?		

3a.

1   What did you do?

2   What happened then?

3   What did he say after that?

4   What did you do then?

3b.

1	When	3	Where
2	What	4	Why

3c.

a

1   When do you usually go? / When is it?

2   What do you usually do?

3   Where do you usually go?

4   Why is that?

b

1   When are you going (to do that)?

2   What are you going to do?

3   Where are you going to go?

4   Why are you going to do that? / Why are you going to go there? / Why is that?

4a.

1   Have you ever *tried* Indian food? Yes, I have.

2   Have you ever *been* to Edinburgh? No, I haven't.

3   Have you ever *worked* with people from China? No, not yet.

Unit 3

2a.
They are talking about national cuisines.

2b.

1	T	3	T	5	T	7	F
2	F	4	F	6	F	8	T

3.

a
You might interrupt someone during a conversation to:
- ask them to repeat something
- ask them to clarify or explain something
- comment or add your own opinion
- agree or disagree with them.

b

a	2, 3, 6, 9	d	1	g	7
b	10	e	4		
c	5	f	8		

4.
1 What do you think
2 you might know this
3 you have some experience of this

5.

1	D	2	ID	3	D	4	ID	5	D

Unit 4

2a.
They are talking about India.

2b.

1	a	2	b	3	b	4	a	5	b

2c.

1	b	2	c	3	a

3.

1	g	3	c, h	5	d, f
2	b, e	4	a, i, j		

4.

1	c	2	a	3	b

Phrases used to introduce the rephrasing:
What I'm trying to say is … / In other words, … / Let me put it another way: …

5.

1	Actually	4	for instance
2	On the whole	5	roughly
3	mostly		

6.
1 I've got to go / It's been nice talking to you / thanks for the chat
2 It's time to start the meeting / we should get down to business
3 I've enjoyed talking to you / it was really interesting thanks

Module 8

Unit 1

1a.
Correct order: Exports, Money, Multiculturalism, Famous singers and writers, The population, The monarchy, Political parties, TV channels, Newspapers

1b.
1 England / Scotland / Wales / Northern Ireland
2 manufactured
3 100 / pound
4 ethnically
5 61 million
6 Conservatives / Labour Party / Liberal Democrats

3a.

1	f	3	c	5	d
2	a	4	e	6	b

3b.
1 Easter
2 Chinese New Year
3 Thanksgiving Day
4 Christmas Day
5 New Year's Eve
6 Ramadan

4a.

Tip 1: UK	Tip 4: Denmark
Tip 2: China	Tip 5: Japan
Tip 3: France	

Unit 2

1a.
Correct order: Non-verbal communication, Facial expressions, Eye contact, Gestures, Negative signals, Misinterpretation

2a.

1	d	2	c	3	e	4	a	5	b

2b.

1	about	4	about
2	on	5	about
3	in		

3a.

a	6	c	3	e	5
b	2	d	1	f	4

3b.

1	d	2	c	3	a	4	b

4b.

a	1	b	3	c	2

Unit 3

1a. /1b.
Safe: the weather / holidays / food
Taboo: sex / religion / politics / salaries
Somewhere in the middle: the economy / the news / a current war / a current business scandal / family

Note: The subjects 'in the middle' could be safe or taboo depending on the sensitivity of the topic and the person you are talking to.

2.

1	in	3	of	5	from
2	to	4	at	6	on

3b.

a	3	b	1	c	4	d	2

4a.

wisecrack 4	punch line 3
pun 1	running gag 5
in-joke 2	

4b.
Pun 1: A person's 'waist' is the middle part of the human body just below the stomach. The waist is often associated with being fat or thin. 'Waist' also sounds the same as 'waste' – which means not using something valuable in an effective way – and rhymes with 'taste', which is the flavour of a food. So the word 'waist' is relevant to losing weight in many ways.

Pun 2: To 'call' means to use the telephone, but to 'call on' means to decide to use something that someone can offer you. So both meanings of the word could be true for a telecommunications company.

Unit 4

2.

1	multi-tasker	2	linear tasker

3b.
1 Spain.
2 Because his Spanish business contact was late for their meeting.
3 He called Juan's mobile.
4 Because he remembered a cultural training course in which he had learnt that many Spanish people have a more laid-back attitude to time and punctuality.

4a.

a	1	b	3	c	2

4b.

i	3	ii	2	iii	1

Module 9

Unit 1

1a.

1	classical	5	rock
2	pop	6	easy listening
3	jazz	7	folk
4	hip hop	8	soul

2a.

| animation 6 |
| romantic comedies 1 |
| musicals 7 |
| sci-fi movies 3 |
| war films 8 |
| horror films 2 |
| period dramas 4 |
| action / thrillers 5 |

3a.
Styles of art: surrealist / impressionist / modern / classical
Words connected with painting: oil / watercolour / canvas / brush / gallery / easel

3b.

1 Angie likes it, Marc dislikes it.
2 Angie dislikes it, Marc likes it.
3 Both dislike it.

4a.

1	e	3	d	5	b
2	f	4	c	6	a

4b.

1 Enduring Love
2 Ian McEwan
3 She can't stop reading it.

Unit 2

1a.

a
1 football and tennis 2 football
b
1 tennis   2 football

1b.

1 Did you see the match last night?
2 Do you follow any sports?
3 Who do you think will win the cup?
4 Who do you support?

2a.

1	rowing	4	athletics
2	sailing	5	basketball
3	weightlifting		

2b.

1 pool (pool is a game, or short for
   'swimming pool'; all the others are
   things you use in order to play a sport)
2 golf (all the others are watersports)
3 platinum (all the others are types of
   Olympic medal)
4 squash (in squash you use a racket; in
   all the others you use just a ball)

3a.

football	1	tennis	4
rugby	6	taekwondo	5
motor racing	2	golf	7
athletics	3	swimming	8

3b.

1	lost, won	3	set
2	nil, points	4	wickets, beat

4a.

1	f	3	c	5	e
2	d	4	a	6	b

Unit 3

1.

Verbs: hear / listen to / catch up with
Adjectives: breaking / latest / financial /
international
Nouns: sports / business

2a.

Economy: credit crunch / downturn
Crime: fraud / tax evasion / kidnap / trial /
hostage / prison
Global warming: climate change /
temperatures
Employment: union / industrial dispute /
strike

2b.

Correct order: Crime, Global warming,
Strike, Columbian kidnap, Finance, The
weather

2c.

1	is	4	free
2	does	5	should not
3	not go ahead	6	good

2d.

1	accused	4	rebel
2	evidence	5	rally
3	backed down	6	forecast

3b.

1	f	3	c	5	g	7	e
2	a	4	b	6	h	8	d

3c.

Students own answers, but as a guide:
- celebrity gossip is usually found in the
  tabloids;
- the other sections are usually found in
  both types of newspaper, although
  coverage is usually more in-depth in the
  broadsheets – particularly in the more
  'serious' areas such as business and
  finance, for example.

Unit 4

1a.

1 interactive whiteboards
2 moving abroad
3 meeting times

1b.

1	emotional	3	rational
2	statistical		

1c.

1 Why don't you …?
2 You have to admit that …
3 Wouldn't you agree that …?
4 Don't you think that …?

2b.

Who? May Bee / Mel Gordon
When? Last night
Where? Mel Gordon's party
What happened? May Bee left the party,
crying
Why? They had an argument

3a.

1	controversial	3	emotional
2	sensitive		

3b.

Correct order: Global warming, ID cards,
Smoking in public places, Digital
downloads

3c.

Phrases used: a, c, d, e, g, h, i, j, l
Brad also says: 'how about we just drop it?'
(informal)

My social planner
Module 1

Unit 1 – Talking about you and your life

1.1 Complete some of the following sentence 'heads' so that they are true for you.

I was born in …   I live in …
I went to school in …   My father / mother is / was a …
I went to …   university.   I have a friend in …
I work for …   My wife / husband / partner is from …
I started work in …   (*year*) We have …   child / children

1.2 Write some sentences about yourself and your life. Use some of the words in the box.

moved   left/quit   trained to be   used to be   graduated   was promoted

_____

_____

_____

Unit 2 – Asking and answering questions

Practise saying the following. Pay attention to stress and intonation. Notice any contractions and weak forms.

What's your name?   Where do you live?   How long have you worked for …?
Where are you from?   What do you do in your free time?   How was your journey?
What do you do?   Who do you work for?   Where are you staying?

Unit 3 – Talking about your company and business

Write sentences about your own company / business. Use some of the words in the box.

founded   subsidiary   HQ   competition   client(s)   turnover   market(s)   expand   won/lost a contract in

_____

_____

_____

Unit 4 – Greetings, introductions and goodbyes

4.1 Decide which expressions are formal. Which do you need to use? Practise saying them aloud.

May I introduce you to …   It's a great pleasure to meet you.   Let me introduce …
Nice to meet you.   This is …   How do you do?

4.2 Write your own answer to the following question.

How's business?

4.3 Tick any of the following words / phrases you use in the business situations you are usually in.

Bye
Catch you later
Goodbye
Ciao

My social planner
Module 2

Unit 1 – Talking about free time and travel

1.1 Hobbies

What do you do when you're not at work? Write some sentences which are true for you.

In my free time, I …   I play …

I've recently taken up …   I collect …

1.2 Places in the world

I love …   (name of country)   I'd love to go to …   (name of country)

Unit 2 – Talking about your town and country

You are playing host to a group of visiting business colleagues. It's the first time they have visited your country. What would you like to tell them? Make notes on the following:

Places to visit in my country:

Places to visit in my town / city:

A famous national dish:

A highlight of my capital city:

A famous person from my country:

A souvenir they should buy:

Unit 3 – Food and drink

3.1 Write in your own answers.

(In a bar) What would you like to drink?

(In a restaurant) What shall we order?

3.2 Complete the sentences so they are true for you.

My favourite dish is …

I love …

I don't usually eat …

3.3 Describe your favourite dish.

_____

_____

3.4 Answer the questions.

Do you drink coffee?   What is your favourite cuisine?

Unit 4 – Talking about jobs and work

4.1 Complete the sentences about your own job.

I'm a …   I'm responsible for …

I work for …   I'm responsible to …

4.2 Answer the questions.

What's your job like?   What do you like about your job?

My social planner
Module 3

Unit 1 – Likes, dislikes and preferences

1.1 Complete these sentence heads with true statements. Choose a relevant topic, for example food / drink / music / hobbies / films.

I love …   I really like …   I like …   I don't like …   I hate …

1.2 Which do you prefer? Write your answers to these questions. Use expressions such as: *I don't like … / I prefer … / Given the choice, I'd prefer …*

working alone / working in a team
meetings in the office / meetings over lunch
starting work early and finishing early / starting work late and finishing late
communicating by email / communicating by telephone

Unit 2 – Invitations: accepting and declining

2.1 Complete these invitations with real-world examples from your personal and/or professional life.

Would you like to …   ?
Would you be interested in …   ?
Are you free on …   ?

2.2 Practise saying the following. Pay attention to stress and intonation.

I'd love to.   I'd like to very much.   That's very kind of you.
I'm afraid I can't.   Sorry, but I can't make it.   I'm afraid I'm not free on …   Unfortunately, I have to …

Unit 3 – Making requests, offers and recommendations

3.1 Asking for help

Write out your requests for help in these situations:

The airline has lost your luggage.   You have a bad headache.
You can't find where to register at a conference.   You want to get some local currency.

3.2 Recommendations

You have been asked to recommend something. Add more situations to the list below which are true for you. Write out your recommendations using the language in the box.

> You should …   You could …   If I were you, I'd …   It would be good to …   Why don't you …?

Situations: sights to visit in your town/city; a good hotel; a website that gives useful information about your country; a souvenir for a husband/wife/partner; a business book to read; a meal; the local drink …

Unit 4 – Opinions, agreeing and disagreeing

Write sentences giving your opinion on some of the areas in the list below. Use the sentence starters from the box to create your sentences.

> I think …   I reckon …   In my opinion …   I feel …   I'm sure that …   I'm convinced that …

today's weather   a business problem   a new law
a political situation   the environment   the state of the economy

My social planner
Module 4

Unit 1 – Going out for a drink

1.1 Write answers which are true for you.

What would you like to drink?   Tea or coffee?
Still or sparkling?   Black or white?

1.2 What's your favourite drink?

I love …

Unit 2 – At a restaurant

2.1 Write answers which are true for you.

What do you fancy?   Have you been to an Indian restaurant before?
Would you like a starter?   Are you a vegetarian?
What would you like for the main course? Do you like spicy food?
Would you like a dessert?   How do you like your steak?

2.2 Local speciality

Is there a local speciality where you come from? Can you describe it? Complete the sentences.

It's called …   It's similar to …
It's made from …   We usually eat it with …

Unit 3 – At a conference

3.1 Create sentences you may need while networking so they are true for you.

I usually go to conferences on …   (*subject*)
I think …   is a great speaker.
I go to trade fairs, such as …

3.2 Language bank

Practise saying these useful conference phrases:

Have you had a good time?   What was the most interesting session?
Have you learnt anything useful?   Did you make any useful contacts?

Unit 4 – Meeting and greeting visitors

4.1 What excuses can you give for being late?

Sorry to keep you waiting, …   _____

_____

_____

4.2 Complete the questions so they are true for you. Then practise asking them.

How was your … (flight / drive / journey)?   How long are you staying?
Is this your first time in …   ?   Where are you staying?
When were you here before?   How are things in …   ?

My social planner
Module 5

Unit 1 – Describing, comparing and talking about the best

1.1 Write a short description of somewhere, someone and something which will help you when networking. For example, answers to these questions:

What's (your office) like?
What's (your boss) like?
What's (your best-selling product) like?

1.2 Compare two:

- hotels
- cities

- cars
- conferences / trade fairs

1.3 Write sentences using the superlative which you might need to say in a networking situation. For example: *It's the best product on the market.*

_____

_____

_____

Unit 2 – Talking about the present and using modals

Complete the sentences with statements which are true for you.

2.1 **Present simple**

I live in …   I work for …

2.2 **Present continuous**

At the moment, I'm working on …   Now, I'm …

2.3 **Modals**

I must / have to …   I should …   I can …

Unit 3 – Talking about the past

Complete the sentences with statements and questions which are true for you.

3.1 **Past simple**

I joined my company in …   How long did you …   ?

3.2 **Present perfect**

I've lived in …   for …   Have you (ever) …   ?
I've lived in …   since …   How long have you …   ?
I've worked for …   for …
I've worked for …   since …

Unit 4 – Talking about the future and speculating

4.1 Complete the sentences with statements which are true for you.

A prediction of how my networking skills will change after using this book: I think …

A plan or intention I have to improve my networking with English: I'm going to …

An appointment or arrangement I want to refer to while socializing: I'm meeting …

4.2 Complete the following to make a question you might use in a networking situation.

What would you do if …   ?

My social planner
Module 6

Unit 1 – Being a good listener

1.1 Suggested strategies to improve your listening include:

DVDs / subtitles	the news on TV	write down some words before a presentation
podcasts	BBC radio news	conversations with native English speakers

1.2 Make notes on your own action plan to improve your listening.

_____

_____

_____

Unit 2 – Listening for the general idea

Task: go on the internet and choose a short clip to listen to. Choose one where you can listen again and use the 'pause' button. Make notes and then write a short summary.
Possible websites: www.bbc.co.uk, www.cnn.com

Unit 3 – Listening for specific information

Create your own list of words to help you with spelling. Remember to use famous towns, countries or words that would be recognized internationally.

A for _____   H for _____   O for _____   V for _____
B for _____   I for _____   P for _____   W for _____
C for _____   J for _____   Q for _____   X for _____
D for _____   K for _____   R for _____   Y for _____
E for _____   L for _____   S for _____   Z for _____
F for _____   M for _____   T for _____
G for _____   N for _____   U for _____

Unit 4 – Listening: pronunciation

4.1 Task: individual sounds

Do you know which sounds are especially problematic for you? Visit the Macmillan website (www.macmillanenglish.com) and download an interactive version of the pronunciation chart, and use it to identify any problem areas.

4.2 Word stress

Write down any words which cause you problems when you say them. Mark the stress. Practise them until you have the right pronunciation.

My social planner
Module 7

Unit 1 – Making small talk

Choose another one of the topics from page 57 exercise 5b and make notes for a short story to tell to a colleague or business associate.

_____

_____

_____

_____

_____

Unit 2 – Active listening

2.1 Review. Practise saying some of these expressions, which can be used when listening to a story. Pay attention to intonation.

Oh yes?	How awful	No!?!	Is that so?
That's a shame	I see	Really?	Right
Go on	That was lucky	That's incredible!	Oh dear

2.2 Use these question words to create more questions to push a story forward. Then practise saying them.

What …	Who …	When …
Which …	Where …	Why …

Unit 3 – Managing a conversation

Choose some of these phrases that you think will be useful. Practise saying them.

Can I say something quickly?	Sorry to interrupt, but I think [Angie] is right.
Sorry to interrupt, but …	Sorry to interrupt, but I'm afraid I don't agree.
Sorry, could I just say, …	Go ahead.
Could I add something here?	Just a moment, let me finish what I was saying.
Sorry to interrupt. Could you explain that?	Please continue.

Unit 4 – Checking and clarifying

Choose some of these phrases that you think will be useful. Practise saying them.

Could you go through that again?	So, in other words, you're saying …?
Sorry, I didn't catch that.	So that's …
Sorry, I'm not with you.	So, if I understand correctly, …
Could you explain?	Oh, that's clear.
Could you explain what you mean?	OK, I see what you mean.

My social planner
Module 8

Unit 1 – Talking about your country: festivals and etiquette

1.1 Complete these categories with any useful information about your country to tell visitors.

Exports: Ruling monarch or head of state:
Currency: Political parties:
Famous people: TV channels:
Population: Newspapers:

1.2 Think about a special date in your own country. Why is this date important?

1.3 Complete this section with some useful etiquette tips for your country.

Business dress:
Exchanging business cards:
Tipping:
Cuisine:
Exchanging gifts:

Unit 2 – Body language

2.1 Make notes on any important aspects of body language which you need to explain to visitors to your country.

gestures   eye contact
personal space   greetings

2.2 Make notes on any important aspects of body language which you need to know about a country you are going to visit on business.

gestures   eye contact
personal space   greetings

Unit 3 – Taboo areas and humour

3.1 Note any taboo areas for visitors to your country.

_____

3.2 Note any useful information on local humour for visitors to your country.

_____

3.3 Write down a joke which could be used in a networking situation.

_____

Unit 4 – Attitudes to time and meetings across cultures

4.1 Make notes on the following topics which visitors to your country should know:

time

meetings etiquette

4.2 Make notes on the following topics which visitors to another country you do business in should know:

time

meetings etiquette

Learning tip: go to www.kwintessential.co.uk for help on this.

My social planner
Module 9

Unit 1 – Talking about the arts

Create sentences which are true for you and will be useful in a networking situation.

1.1   Talking about music.

My favourite band is …

My favourite singer is …

My favourite song is …

My favourite album is …

1.2   Talking about films

Write down information about a film you like.

Title:

Director:

Stars:

Why I like this particular film:

The story is set in …

It's about …

In the end …

1.3   Talking about art

What is the name of your favourite painting? Why do you like it?

1.4   Talking about books

What is one of your favourite books? Why?

Unit 2 – Talking about sport

2.1   Useful questions:

Did you see the match last night?   Do you follow/play any sports?   Who do you support?

2.2   Complete any of these phrases which you would like to use:

I play …

I used to play …

I like …

I love …

I'm a fan of …

I have just taken up …

Unit 3 – Talking about news and the media

3.1   Useful conversation-starting phrases

Have you heard about …?   Did you hear the news this morning?

3.2   My media

Where do you get your news from? Complete the sentence starters so they are true for you.

TV: I often watch …

Newspapers: I usually read …

Magazines: I usually read …

Radio: I often listen to …

Internet: I love reading …

Blogs: I read …

Unit 4 – Persuading and handling controversial topics

Write down the subject of a situation where you have to persuade someone to your point of view.

Now, complete these sentence starters with your arguments:

You have to admit that …

Wouldn't you agree that …

Don't you think that …